I0119975

James L Bennett

Plants of Rhode Island

James L Bennett

Plants of Rhode Island

ISBN/EAN: 9783744734271

Printed in Europe, USA, Canada, Australia, Japan

Cover: Foto ©Andreas Hilbeck / pixelio.de

More available books at **www.hansebooks.com**

PROCEEDINGS OF PROVIDENCE FRANKLIN SOCIETY.

PLANTS

OF

RHODE ISLAND,

BEING

AN ENUMERATION

OF

PLANTS GROWING WITHOUT CULTIVATION

IN THE STATE

OF

RHODE ISLAND,

(*Latitude 41° 18' to 42° 3' N.*)
(*Longitude 71° 8' to 71° 53' W.*)

"NOMINA SI NESCIS, PERIT COGNITIO RERUM."

BY

JAMES L. BENNETT.

PROVIDENCE, R. I.
PROVIDENCE PRESS COMPANY, PRINTERS.
1888.

At a regular meeting of the Providence Franklin Society, January 6, 1885, the Standing Committee was authorized to print reports on Botany and Geology.

Attest: JOHN DABOLL,

Secretary.

BOTANICAL COMMITTEE:

Mr. GEORGE HUNT,

" THOMAS J. BATTEY,

" D. W. HOYT,

Mrs. E. M. ALDEN.

It is now more than forty years since the publication of Mr. Olney's Catalogue of Rhode Island Plants,* which was the first enumeration, other than the partial lists occasionally made by visiting botanists, ever made of our plants. Since that time, and more especially during the last decade, the study of Botany has received increased attention, and is regularly taught in the schools, generally, however, in a merely perfunctory and necessarily superficial manner, but any attention given to the study is an advance upon the previous total neglect of the science. The Franklin Society has continued its discussions and lectures upon botanical subjects, and an interest has been maintained and fostered, which, it is pleasant to note, is more general at the present than at any previous time; withal, Mr. Olney's generous bequest to Brown University, and the endowment of a professorship of Botany under his will, has made the possibility of gaining a knowledge of botanical science so comparatively easy, that it is but reasonable to expect that this branch of Biology is to receive, at least in part, that attention which it deserves.

When the first enumeration was made, many problems remained unsolved which are to-day of easy explanation; text books to which recourse might be had for careful generalizations from

* *The first part of this Catalogue was the conjoined work of the Committee of the Providence Franklin Society, Stephen T. Olney, George Hunt, George Thurber and Henry B. Metcalf; the supplementary additions were made by Mr. Olney.*

accumulated observation, were in more than one direction at that time entirely lacking; sources now broadly open to all were then, so far as they at all existed, accessible to none other than the professional botanist; new fields prolific in unimagined forms were all around us, but for long time we were entirely dependent upon our older brothers beyond the sea (with whom correspondence was frequently in a foreign tongue), for information and knowledge. which is now the privilege of the beginner.

It is not then strange that the first enumeration of Rhode Island plants contained but one-third as many as we note in the following list, which itself contains, it is believed, but little more than the half of those species which grow without cultivation within our borders.

This Catalogue is prepared at the suggestion of and under the auspices of the Providence Franklin Society, and forms a portion of its published proceedings. It has in large measure been compiled for a number of years, but for many reasons its issue has postponed; yet we trust that the larger field which it consequently covers will make amends for the delay, especially as we are thereby enabled to add several hundred species.

The list could have been never made, certainly not to embrace so much of the field which it aims to cover, without kindly and very generous aid of many friends, all of whom will understand, we trust, that whether their names appear in its pages or not, the sense of obligation is here fully acknowledged and thankfully remembered.

It would be impossible to mention all those who have in various ways, by advice or suggestion or information, contributed to any measure of success attained, yet it were unworthy not to acknowledge an indebtedness, for many years in common with every botanist, to him who for so long time was "*facile princeps*" of botanists, and kindliest of men; on whom we were in so many ways dependent, who was so entirely our wise leader and teacher, that we ever refused to think of that time when he might be called away from us. The importance biological studies now hold in American schools and colleges and in an enlightened public esteem, and the value therefrom which results to every commonwealth, is due more than to any other to DR. ASA GRAY.

> "All hearts grew warmer in the presence
> Of him who, seeking not his own,
> Gave freely,—for the love of giving,
> Nor reaped for self the harvest sown."

May the memory of his simple, unaffected life, full of wisdom and the desire to be helpful, linger long with us and strengthen us, according to our degree, to similar loving acts of help !

We have to thank for assistance in special departments Mr. William Boott, for kind aid in the nomenclature of the genus *Carex ;* Dr. George Thurber and Dr. George Vasey for similar aid in *Gramineæ ;* Mr. Willey, of New Bedford, for revision of the *Lichenes ;* Dr. W. G. Farlow, of Cambridge, and Prof. D. C. Eaton, of New Haven, for many additions to the list of *Marine Algæ ;* Mr. C. H. Peck, of Albany, N. Y., and Mr. J. B. Ellis, of Newfield, N. J., for revision of the *Fungi ;* Mr. L. Lesquereux, for the naming and verification of many species of *Musci ;* Rev. Francis Wolle, for information regarding *Fresh Water Algæ ;* Mr. Lathrop, for contribution of *Desmidiaceæ,* &c. ; and other friends whose contributions are noted in the text. Thanks are due to the Botanical Committee of the Franklin Society, for their patience and consideration in the extremely vexatious delays which have occurred, and especially for the liberal manner in which they have provided for the publication of these pages.

Gray's Manual—5th edition, 1867—has been followed in the arrangement and nomenclature of the *Flowering Plants and Ferns,* and in those cases where by proper authority such names have been reformed, the former name is inserted in *italics*.

Dr. Vasey's various publications have determined the arrangement, &c., of *Gramineæ ;*[1] Lesquereux' and James' that of the *Musci ;*[2] the late Prof. Tuckerman the *Lichenes ;*[3] Mr. M. C. Cooke's arrangement of the *Fungi*[4] has been followed, with revisions by Mr. Peck and Mr. Ellis; Dr. Farlow has been the guide for the *Marine Algæ,*[5] and Rev. Mr. Wolle for the *Fresh Water Algæ.*[6] It should be noted that for convenience' sake the *Marine* and *Fresh Water Algæ* are separated, and in the one is followed Dr. Farlow's ascending, and in the other Mr. Wolle's descending series. Although unscientific, it was believed that there were sufficient advantages in not merging all the *Algæ* under one systematic arrangement. The arrangement of the *Diatomaceæ*[7] is that in Pritchard. We follow Prof. Underwood's arrangement of *Hepaticæ.*[8]

The *Musci* were determined or previous determinations verified by Mr. Lesquereux. Some of them, however, and all the Hepaticæ, passed through the hands of the late Mr. Coe F. Austin.

The late Prof. Tuckerman very kindly determined, or verified, the *Lichenes*, and all herein named passed under his examination. The *Fungi* were all named by the late Rev. Dr. M. A. Curtis, or by him in connection with Dr. Berkely; the revision of the same by

[1] Descriptive Catalogue of United States Grasses, 1884.

[2] Manual of the Mosses of North America, 1884.

[3] Synopsis of N. Am. Lichens. Part 1. 1882. Genera Lichenum, 1872.

[4] Handbook of British Fungi, 1871.

[5] List of the Marine Algæ of the United States, 1875. Marine Algæ of New England and adjacent coast, 1881, &c.

[6] Desmids of the United States, 1884, and Supplement, 1887. Fresh Water Algæ of the United States, 1887.

[7] Pritchard's Infusoria, 1861. Article Diatomaceæ.

[8] Descriptive Catalog of the North American Hepaticæ, north of Mexico, 1885.

Mr. Peck and Mr. Ellis has been referred to. Valuable assistance was received from Mr. Olney's *Algæ Rhodiaceæ*, to which reference is duly made by No. in the text, and wherever the names have been reformed, the species as named in *Alg. Rhod.* follows the now accepted name in *italics*. Very valuable information regarding a large number of *Diatoms* was obtained from Mr. S. A. Briggs' papers in The Lens.

A great amount of material in *Desmids, Diatoms*, &c., await determination, and all our fresh water pools, and ponds, and brooks, teem with species yet to us unknown.

·

It has been the intention to insert the names of all plants so far found indigenous to the State, and also all those not native, but which have become thoroughly naturalized; the names of all plants which did not appear to be perfectly established, are omitted ; unquestionably there are some which deserve insertion, and further study will allow their claim, but " consuetudo loci observando est," and it has been thought better to practice that conservatism which has heretofore characterized Rhode Island's treatment of aliens, and make them fully earn citizenship before allowing it. Naturalized plants are designated in the text by the method of spacing commonly adopted.

Wherever the habitat is general it is not mentioned, but when the plant has been found only locally, such fact is noted; when a species has been noted by only one collector, such fact is stated, save that in a few cases the note refers to the person by whom it was first found; the other notes will explain themselves. These remarks do not apply to the *Cryptogamia*, as the marine algæ were worked out first by Mr. Olney, and the other orders mainly by the writer.

Although this enumeration contains the names of upwards of 3,150 species and varieties, yet it is probably only the moiety of those which grow in the State. The *Phanerogams* and *Acrogens* are pretty nearly full, the *Anophytes* less so, but no department of the *Thallogens*, except the *Marine Algæ*, is probably represented in this list by one-half of those species which belong there; indeed, the enumeration was so evidently incomplete, that at first it was intended to omit the entire class, except the *Marine Algæ*, and it is now inserted with this explanation, and the hope that microscopists may be induced to search out and add the missing species to those herein named.

It may well be said in this connection, that questions of greatest interest, not alone in a merely technical sense, await solution, which may fairly be expected from the study of the life history of the microscopic *Algæ* and allies: that algoid and fungoid vegetation has much to do with disease in man and beast and higher vegetable organisms, is held as proven; but whether as cause or effect, or only coincident, is not entirely agreed. No greater questions of material value await determination, than the relations between decay of physical life and the growth of microscopic vegetation. It may be perhaps that the study of these relations, by some of our younger botanists shall lead to an elucidation of facts and a determination of truths of unmeasured value to the commonwealth.

That family of plants, *Protophyta*, containing those species always present in *ferments*, comprising *Saccharomyces, Bacillus, Bacterium*, &c., is not here noted; a lack which some future student must supply.

All that is claimed for this enumeration is its purpose to help and encourage the beginner; — at the same time it gives, we believe, correct information to the advanced botanist of facts regarding habitats and distribution of species. Claim to absolute accuracy of determination, in every case, is not made, and it is frankly admitted that corrections, as well as reformations, perhaps not a few, may be necessary. Information of necessary additions or corrections is desired.

Criticism of the manner in which the work has been done may be deserved; there can fairly be none, however, of the intent, which is, to magnify the wonders of Nature, and prompt the student, to look beyond *Nature's merely outward appearing.*

Whatever of value the following pages possess belongs in largest measure to the help of kind friends ; whatever of incorrectness and imperfection to the writer.

JAMES L. BENNETT.

PROVIDENCE, September 1, 1888.

CORRECTIONS AND ADDITIONS.

Page 4, l. 12. Add **Alyssum incanum**, L. Providence, J. L. B.
" 5, " 26. For **tomentesa**, read **tomentosa**.
" 7, " 8. " **Spurrer**, read **spurge**.
" 7, " 17. " **Perlslane**, read **Purslane**.
" 10, " 5. Add **Genista tinctoria**, L. Newport, Tweedy.
" 12, " 8. Add **Poterium Canadense**, L. Matunuck, J. L. B.
" 16, " 2. For Beuth, read Benth.
" " " 26. " **ÆGAPODIUM**, read **ÆGOPODIUM**.
" 21, " 35. " WORMWEED, read WORMWOOD.
" 22, " 22. " Rinz, read Ruiz.
" 23, " 15. " **oboyatus**, read **obovatus**.
" " " 30 and 32. For Scap, read Scop.
" 24, " 1. For **Cateen**, read **Cotton**.
" 27, " 10. " **DISPYROS**, read **DIOSPYROS**.
" 30, " 3. Add **Rhinanthus Crista-Galli**, L. Newport, Tweedy.
" 34. Before Order 66, insert
ORDER **NYCTAGINACEÆ**.
Oxybaphus nyctagineus, Sweet. E. Providence, Arnold Green, Esq.
" 35, " 13. For SAMPHINE, read SAMPHIRE.
" 36, " 6. Add **P. Pennsylvanicum**, L. Common.
" 40, " 24. For Peir, read Poir.
" " " 25. " Caw, read Carr.
" 44, " 6. " **verticellata**, read **verticillata**.
" " " 34. " **auceps**, read **anceps**.
" 46, " 19. " BAY, read BOG.
" 51, " 17. " **microcarpum**, read **microcarpon**.
" " " 22 and 24. For C. read P.
" 54, " 48. For PHRAGMITIS, read PHRAGMITES.
" 57, " 3. " **Ebeneum**, read **ebeneum**.
" 58, " 35. " **septentrionavis**, read **septentrionalis**.
" " " 27. Add var. **gracilis**, Engelm. Larkin's Pond.
" 61, " 4. For Hcau, read Hedw.
" " " 30. " Sebth, read Sibth.

Page 62, l. 12.   For Sebwægr, read Schwægr.
  "   73, " 44.   " **Duræii**, read **Duriæi.**
  "   77, " 31.   " **foensecii**, read **foenisecii.**
  "   80, " 11.   " **brunalis**, read **brumalis.**
  "   95, " 6.   " **LYNGBIA**, read **LYNGBYA.**
  " 100, " 12.   Add No. 44.
  "   ·· " 16.   Add No. 42.
  " 103, " 26.   For *Sphærrophea*, read *Sphæroplea.*
  " 104, " 6.   " **RHIZOZLONIUM**, read **RHIZOCLO-NIUM.**
  " 108 and 109.   For Ehrh. wherever it occurs, read Ehrb.
  " 111, l. 15.   For Thwaiter, read Thwaites.
  " 112, " 3.   Add var. **Crux-Africanum**, Wolle.   Cat Swamp.

SERIES I.

PHÆNOGAMIA.

Class I. DICOTYLEDONEÆ.

Sub-Class I. ANGIOSPERMÆ.

Division I. POLYPETALÆ.

Order 1. **RANUNCULACEÆ.**

CLEMATIS, L. Virgin's Bower.
1. **verticillaris, D. C.**   Johnston.
2. **Virginiana, L.**

ANEMONE, L. Wind-flower.
1. **cylindrica,** Gray.
2. **Virginiana, L.**
3. **nemorosa, L.**
4. **Hepatica, L.,** var. **obtusiloba.**
    Hepatica triloba, Chaix.

ANEMONELLA, Spach.

thalictroides, Spach.
    Thalictrum anemonoides Michx.

THALICTRUM, Tourn. Meadow-Rue.
1. **purpurascens, L.**
2. **dioicum, L.**
3. **Cornuti, L.**

RANUNCULUS, L. Crowfoot, Buttercup.
1. **aquatilis, L.,** var. **trichophyllus,** Chaix.
2. **multifidus,** Pursh.
3. **alismæfolius,** Geyer.   Little Compton.
4. **Flammula, L.,** var. **reptans,** Gray.   N. Providence.
5. **Cymbalaria,** Pursh.
6. **abortivus, L.**
7. **recurvatus,** Poiret.
8. **Pennsylvanicus, L.**
9. **fascicularis,** Muhl.
10. **repens, L.**

11. **bulbosus,** L.
12. **acris,** L.

        CALTHA, L. MARSH MARIGOLD.
palustris, L.

        COPTIS, Salisb. GOLDTHREAD.
trifolia, Salisb.

        AQUILEGIA, L. COLUMBINE.
Canadensis, L.

        ACTÆA, L. COHOSH.
1. **spicata,** L., var. **rubra,** Michx.
2. **alba,** Bigelow.

        CIMICIFUGA, L. BLACK SNAKEROOT.
racemosa, Ell.

      ORDER 2. **MAGNOLIACEÆ.**
    LIRIODENDRON, L. TULIP-TREE.
Tulipifera, L.

      ORDER 3. **BERBERIDACEÆ.**
      BERBERIS, L. BARBERRY.
vulgaris, L.

CAULOPHYLLUM, Michx. PAPPOOSE-ROOT.
thalictroides, Michx.   Cumberland, *Olney.*   Smithfield,
  Battey.

      PODOPHYLLUM, L. MAY-APPLE.
peltatum, L.   Hopkinton, *Bennett.*

      ORDER 4. **NYMPHÆACEÆ.**
      BRASENIA, Schreb. WATER-SHIELD.
peltata, Pursh.

      NYMPHÆA. POND-LILY.
odorata, Ait.
      var. **minor.**
      var. **rosea.** Warwick, *Dr. George Thurber, Bennett.*

      NUPHAR, Smith. SPATTER-DOCK.
advena, Ait.

ORDER 5.　**SARRACENIACEÆ.**

SARRACENIA, Tourn.　SIDE-SADDLE FLOWER.
purpurea, L.

ORDER 6.　**PAPAVERACEÆ.**

CHELIDONIUM, L.　CELANDINE.
majus, L.

SANGUINARIA, Dill.　BLOOD-ROOT.
Canadensis, L.

GLAUCIUM, Tourn.　HORN-POPPY.
luteum, Scop.

ORDER 7.　**FUMARIACEÆ.**

ADLUMIA, Raf.

cirrhosa, Raf.　Cumberland, rare.　　　　Foster. *Flint.*

CORYDALIS, Vent.
glauca, Pursh.

FUMARIA, L.　FUMITORY.
officinalis, L.　An occasional weed.

ORDER 8.　**CRUCIFERÆ.**

NASTURTIUM, R. Br.　CRESS.
1. officinale, R. Br.
2. palustre, D. C.
3. Armoracia, Fries.　HORSE-RADISH.

CARDAMINE, L.　LADY'S-SMOCK.
1. rhomboidea, D. C.
2. hirsuta, L.
　　　var. sylvatica, Gray.

ARABIS, L.　ROCK-CRESS.
1. lævigata, D. C.
2. Canadensis, L.
3. perfoliata, Lam.

BARBAREA, R. Br.　WINTER-CRESS.
vulgaris, R. Br.

ERYSIMUM, L. TREACLE-MUSTARD.

cheiranthoides, L.   Providence.

SISYMBRIUM, L. HEDGE-MUSTARD.

1. **officinale**, Scop.
2. **Sophia**, L.   *J. L. Bennett.*

BRASSICA, Tourn. MUSTARD.

1. **Sinapistrum**, Boiss.
2. **alba**, Boiss.
3. **nigra**, Boiss.

DRABA, L* WHITLOW-GRASS.

1. **Caroliniana**, Walt.
2. **verna**, L.

CAMELINA, Cranz. FALSE-FLAX.

Sativa, Crantz.

CAPSELLA, Vent. SHEPHERD'S-PURSE.

Bursa-Pastoris, Moench.

THLASPI, Tourn. PENNY-CRESS.

arvense, L. E. Providence, *A. Greene, Esq.* Providence,
Bennett.

LEPIDIUM, L. PEPPER-WORT.

1. **Virginianum**, L.
2. **ruderale**, L.
3. **campestre**, L.
4. **Draba**, L.

SENEBIERA, D. C. WART-CRESS.

1. **Coronopus**, D. C.   Newport, *Bennett.*
2. **didyma**, Pers.   Newport, *Bennett.*

CAKILE, Tourn. SEA-ROCKET.

Americana, Nutt.

RAPHANUS, L. RADISH.

1. **Raphanistrum**, L.
2. **sativum**, L. Occasionally spontaneous.

ORDER 9. **RESEDACEÆ.**

RESEDA, L. MIGNONETTE.

Luteola, L. Wanskuck, *Olney.* DYERS-WEED.

---

* *Alyssum maritimum*, L. is (rarely) spontaneous.

ORDER 10. VIOLACEÆ.
VIOLA, L. VIOLET.

1. rotundifolia, Michx.   Burrillville, *Bennett.*
2. lanceolata, L.
3. primulæfolia, L.
4. blanda, Willd, & var.
5. odorata, L.
6. palmata, L.
     V. cucullata, var. palmata.
          var. cucullata.
     V. cucullata, Ait.
7. sagittata, Ait., & vars.*
8. pedata, L.
          var. bicolor.   *Bailey, Bennett.*
9. canina, L., var. Muhlenbergii, Gray.
          V. canina, var. sylvestris, Regel.
10. striata, Ait.
11. pubescens, Ait.
          var. scabriuscula. *Dr. George Thurber.* Providence, *Bennett.*

ORDER 11. CISTACEÆ.
HELIANTHEMUM, Tourn. ROCK-ROSE.

Canadensis, Michx. ICE-WORT.

HUDSONIA, L.

1. ericoides, L.
2. tomentesa, Nutt.

LECHEA, L. PIN-WEED.

1. major, Michx.
2. thymifolia, Pursh.
3. minor, Lam., var. racemulosa.
          var. tenuifolia.
4. Novæ-Cæsareæ, Austin.   Quidnesset, *Bennett.*

ORDER 12. DROSERACEÆ.
DROSERA, L. SUN-DEW.

1. rotundifolia, L.
2. intermedia, Hayne, var. Americanum, D. C.
          D. longifolia, L.

ORDER 13. HYPERICACEÆ.
HYPERICUM, L. ST. JOHN'S-WORT.

1. adpressum. Barton.
2. ellipticum, Hook.

* A variety with fragrant white flowers occurs at Quidnessett.

3. **perforatum**, L.
4. **corymbosum**, Muhl.
5. **mutilum**, L.
6. **Canadense**, L.
   var. **major.**
7. **Sarothra**, Mich. PINE-WEED.

ELODES, Adans.
campanulata. Pursh.
E. Virginica, Arn.

ORDER 14. ELATINACEÆ.
ELATINE, L. WATER-WORT.
Americana, Arnott.

ORDER 15. CARYOPHYLLACEÆ.
DIANTHUS, L. PINK.
Armeria, L.

SAPONARIA, L. SOAPWORT.
officinalis, L.

VACCARIA, Medik. COW-HERB.
vulgaris, Host.

SILENE, L. CATCHFLY.
1. **stellata**, Ait.
2. **inflata**, Sm. BLADDER-CAMPION.
3. **Pennsylvanica**, Michx.   Apponaug, &c.
4. **antirrhina**, L.
5. **noctiflora**, L.   Providence.

LYCHNIS, Tourn.
1. **vespertina**, Sibth.
2. **Githago**, Lam. COCKLE.
3. **diurna**, L.   Providence, &c.

ARENARIA, L. SANDWORT.
1. **serpyllifolia**, L.
2. **Grœnlandica**, Spreng.   Westerly, *Mr. George Hunt.*
3. **laterifolia**, L.
4. **peploides**, L.

STELLARIA, L. STARWORT.
1. **media**, Sm. CHICK-WEED.
2. **longifolia**, Muhl.
3. **borealis**, Bigelow.

CERASTIUM, L. Mouse-Ear Chickweed.

1. **vulgatum**, L.
2. **viscosum**, L.
3. **arvense**, L.   Cumberland. Providence, *Bennett.*

     SAGINA, L. Pearlwort.

1. **procumbens**, L.
2. **apetala**, L.

     LEPIGONIUM, Fries. Sand-Spurrer.

1. **rubrum**, Fries.
         Spergularia rubra, Presl.
2. **salinum**, Fries. (?)
         Spergularia salina, Presl.
3. **medium**, Fries.
         Spergularia media, Presl.

     SPERGULA, L. Spurrey.

arvensis, L.

     Order 16. **PORTULACACEÆ.**

     PORTULACA, Tourn. Perlslane.

oleracea, L.

     CLAYTONIA, L. Spring-Beauty.

Virginica, L.   S. Kingstown, *Olney.*

     Order 17. **MALVACEÆ.**

     MALVA, L. Mallows.

1. **rotundifolia**, L.
2. **sylvestris**, L.
3. **crispa**, L.
4. **moschata**, L.

     ABUTILON, Tourn. Indian Mallow.

Avicennæ, Gærtn.

     HIBISCUS, L.

1. **Trionum**, L.   *Arnold Greene, Esq.*
2. **Syriacus**, L.   S. Kingstown. *J. W. Congdon, Esq.*
3. **Moscheutos**, L.

     Order 18. **TILIACEÆ.**

     TILIA, L. Linden Basswood.

Americana, L. Wick-up Tree.

ORDER 19. **LINACEÆ.**

LINUM, L. FLAX.

1. **Virginianum**, L.
2. **striatum**, Walt.
3. **sulcatum**, Riddell.
4. **usitatissimum**, L., frequent on waste-heaps.

ORDER 20. **GERANIACEÆ.**

GERANIUM, L. CRANE'S-BILL.

1. **maculatum**, L.
2. **Carolinianum**, L.
3. **dissectum**, L.
4. **Robertianum**, L.

ERODIUM, L'Her. STORK'S-BILL.
cicutarium, L'Her.

IMPATIENS, L. BALSAM.

1. **pallida**, Nutt.
2. **fulva**, Nutt. JEWEL-WEED.

OXALIS, L. WOOD-SORRELL.

1. **Acetosella**, L.
2. **violacea**, L.
3. **corniculata**, L., var. **stricta.**
                    O. stricta, L.

ORDER 21. **RUTACEÆ.**

ZANTHOXYLUM, Colden. PRICKLY ASH.
Americanum, Mill.

ORDER 22. **ANACARDIACEÆ.**

RHUS, L. SUMACH.

1. **typhina**, L.
2. **glabra**, L.
3. **copallina**, L.
4. **venenata**, L. SWAMP SUMACH. DOGWOOD.
5. **Toxicodendron**, L. POISON IVY. POISON OAK.
                    var. **radicans.**

ORDER 23. **VITACEÆ.**

VITIS, Tournf. GRAPE.

1. **Labrusca**, L. FOX GRAPE.

2. æstivalis, Michx. SUMMER GRAPE.
3. cordifolia, Michx. FROST GRAPE. E. Providence, &c.
4. riparia, Michx. FROST GRAPE. N. Kingstown; E. Greenwich.

AMPELOPSIS, Michx. VIRGINIA CREEPER.
quinquefolia, Michx.

ORDER 24. **RHAMNACEÆ**.

RHAMNUS, Tourn. BUCKTHORN.
catharticus, L.

CEANOTHUS, L. JERSEY-TEA.
Americanus, L.

ORDER 25. **CELASTRACEÆ**.

CELASTRUS, L. BITTER SWEET.
scandens, L.

ORDER 26. **SAPINDACEÆ**.

STAPHYLEA, L. BLADDER NUT.
trifolia, L. Buck-Hill woods, *Bennett.*

ACER, Tourn. MAPLE.
1. Pennsylvanicum, L. Cumberland, Burrillville.
2. spicatum, Lam. Exeter, *Bennett.*
3. saccharinum, Wang. SUGAR-MAPLE.
        var. **nigrum**.
4. rubrum, L.
5. dasycarpum, Ehrh. Smithfield, &c.

NEGUNDO, Moench. BOX ELDER.
aceroides, Moench. E. Greenwich, *Bennett.*

ORDER 27. **POLYGALACEÆ**.

POLYGALA, Tourn. MILKWORT.
1. sanguinea, L.
2. Nuttallii, T. & G.
3. cruciata, L.
4. brevifolia, Nutt. Apponaug, *Olney, Dr. Robbins.*
5. verticillata, L.
6. Senega, L. SENEGA SNAKE ROOT. *Olney.*
7. polygama, Walt.
8. paucifolia, Willd.

ORDER 28. **LEGUMINOSÆ.**

LUPINUS, Tourn. LUPINE.
perennis, L.

CROTALARIA, L. RATTLE BOX.
sagittalis, L.

TRIFOLIUM, L. CLOVER.
1. arvense, L.
2. pratense, L.
3. medium, L.
4. hybridum, L.
5. repens, L.
6. agrarium, L.
7. procumbens, L.

MELILOTUS, Tourn. MELILOT. SWEET CLOVER.
1. officinalis, Willd.
2. alba, Lam.

MEDICAGO, L. MEDICK.
1. sativa, L. LUCERNE. Sometimes spontaneous (?)
2. lupulina, L.
3. maculata, Willd.
4. denticulata, L.

LOTUS.
siliquosus, L.   Newport, *Bennett.*

ROBINIA, L. ACACIA.
1. Pseudacacia, L.
2. hispida, L. ROSE-ACACIA. Fully established at Quinsnaket.

TEPHROSIA, Pers.
Virginiana, Pers. GOAT'S RUE. CATGUT.

DESMODIUM, D. C. TICK TREFOIL.
1. nudiflorum, D. C.
2. acuminatum, D. C.
3. rotundifolium, D. C.
4. humifusum, Beck.   N. Providence, Johnston.
5. canescens, D. C.   Warwick, *Congdon.*
6. cuspidatum, T. & G.
7. Dillenii, Darlington.
8. paniculatum, D. C.
9. Canadense, D. C.   Davisville, &c.
10. sessilifolium, T. & G. E. Greenwich, *Congdon,* Apponaug, *Bennett.*

11. **rigidum**, D. C.
12. **ciliare**, D. C.
13. **Marilandicum**, Boott.

LESPEDEZA, Michx. BUSH-CLOVER.

1. **procumbens**, Michx.
2. **violacea**, Pers.
3. **Stuvei**, Nutt.
4. **hirta**, Ell.
   forma **unifoliolata**. Quidnessett, *Bennett.*
5. **capitata**, Michx.
   var. **angustifolia**. Davisville, *Bennett.*

VICIA, Tourn. VETCH.

1. **s a t i v a**, L.
2. **t e t r a s p e r m a**, L. Newport, *Bennett.*
3. **Cracca**, L.

LATHYRUS, L. VETCHLING.

1. **maritimus**, Bigelow. BEACH PEA.
2. **palustris**, L.

APIOS, Boerhaave.

tuberosa, Moench. GROUND-NUT.

PHASEOLUS, L. BEAN.

diversifolia, Pers.

AMPHICARPÆA, Ell. HOG PEANUT.

monoica, Nutt.

BAPTISIA, Vent. FALSE INDIGO.

tinctoria, R. Br.

CASSIA, L. SENNA.

1. **Marilandica**, L.
2. **Chamæcrista**, L. PARTRIDGE-PEA.
3. **nictitans**, L. WILD SENSITIVE-PLANT.

GLEDITSCHIA, L. HONEY-LOCUST.

triacanthos, L. Spontaneous.

ORDER 29. ROSACEÆ.

PRUNUS, Tourn. PLUM. CHERRY.

1. **Americana**, Marshall. N. Kingstown, &c.
2. **maritima**, Wang. BEACH-PLUM.
3. **s p i n o s a**, L. BLACK THORN. *J. W. Congdon. Esq.*

4. **pumila,** L. Dwarf Cherry.
5. **Pennsylvanica,** L. Wild Red Cherry.
6. **Virginica,** L. Choke Cherry.
7. **serotina,** Ehrh. Wild Black Cherry.

SPIRÆA, L.

1. **salicifolia,** L. Meadow Sweet.
2. **tomentosa,** L. Hardhack.

AGRIMONIA, Tourn. Agrimony.

Eupatoria, L.

GEUM, L. Avens.

1. **album,** Gmelin.
2. **Virginianum,** L.
3. **strictum,** Ait.
4. **˚rivale,** L.

POTENTILLA, L. Five-Finger.

1. **fruticosa,** L.   Westerly, &c., *Bennett·*
2. **Norvegica,** L.
3. **Canadensis,** L.
         var. **simplex,** T. & G.
4. **argentea,** L.
5. **Anserina,** L.
6. **recta,** L.   Providence, *C. E. Bennett, Prof. Bailey.*

FRAGARIA, Tourn. Strawberry.

1. **Virginiana,** Ehrh.
2. **vesca,** L.

RUBUS, Tourn. Blackberry. Raspberry.

1. **odoratus,** L. Flowering Blackberry.
2. **triflorus,** Richardson. Dwarf Raspberry.
3. **strigosus,** Michx. Red Raspberry.
4. **occidentalis,** L.* Thimbleberry.
5. **villosus,** Ait. High Blackberry.
6. **Canadensis,** L. Low Blackberry.
7. **hispidus,** L. Swamp Blackberry.
8. **Dalibarda.**   Burrillville, *Bennett.*
         Dalibarda, repens, L.

ROSA, Tourn. Rose.

1. **Carolina,** L. Swamp Rose.
2. **lucida,** Ehrhart. Dwarf Wild Rose.
3. **rubiginosa,** L. Sweet Brier.
4. **micrantha,** Sm. Small Flowered Rose.

*A yellow fruited var. is found at Quidnessett.

CRATÆGUS, L. Thorn.

1. **Oxyacantha**, L. Hawthorn.
2. **coccinea**, L. Scarlet Thorn.
3. **tomentosa**, L., var. **pyrifolia**. Pear Thorn.
   var. **punctata**.
4. **Crus-Galli**, L.

PIRUS, L. Chokeberry.

1. **arbutifolia**, L., var. **erythrocarpa**.   Quidnessett, &c.
   var. **melanocarpa**.
2. **Americana**, D. C. Mountain Ash.   Burrillville.

AMELANCHIER, Medik. Shad-Flower.

Canadensis, T. & G. var. **Botryapium**.
              var. **oblongifolia**.
              var. **rotundifolia**.

Order 30. SAXIFRAGACEÆ.

RIBES, L.

1. **oxycanthoides**, L. Gooseberry.
   R. hirtellum, Michx.
2. **floridum**, L. Wild Black Currant.

PARNASSIA, Tourn. Grass of Parnassus.

Caroliniana, Michx.

SAXIFRAGA, L. Saxifrage.

1. **Virginiensis**, Michx.
2. **Pennsylvanica**, L.

CHRYSOSPLENIUM, Tourn. Golden Saxifrage.

Americanum, Schwein.

Order 31. CRASSULACEÆ.

PENTHORUM, Gronov. Dutch Stone-Crop.

sedoides, L.

SEDUM, Tourn. Stone-Crop.

acre, L.
Telephium, L. Live-for-ever.

Order 32. HAMAMELACEÆ.

HAMAMELIS, L. Witch-Hazel.

Virginica, L.

ORDER 33. HALORAGEÆ.

MYRIOPHYLLUM, Vaill. WATER MILFOIL.

1. spicatum, L.   Long Pond, Providence.
2. scabratum, Michx.
3. ambiguum, Nutt.   Providence.
    var. limosum.   Quidnessett.
    var. natans.
    var. capillaceus.   Providence, &c.
4. tenellum, Bigelow.

CALLITRICHE, L. WATER STAR-WORT.

1. verna, L.
2. heterophylla, Pursh.   Hunt's river, Congdon.

PROSERPINACA, L. MERMAID-WEED.

1. palustris, L.
2. pectinacea, Lam.

ORDER 34. ONAGRACEÆ.

CIRCÆA, Tourn. ENCHANTER'S NIGHTSHADE.

1. Lutetiana, L.
2. alpina, L.

EPILOBIUM, L. WILLOW-HERB.

1. spicatum, Lam.
      E. angustifolium, L.
2. h i r s u t u m, L.
3. palustre, L., var. lineare.
4. molle, Torr.
5. coloratum, Muhl.

ŒNOTHERA, L. EVENING-PRIMROSE.

1. biennis, L., & vars.
2. fruticosa, L.   Seekonk, *A. Greene, Esq.*
3. pumila, L.

LUDWIGIA, L. FALSE LOOSESTRIFE.

1. alternifolia, L. SEED-BOX.
2. palustris, L.

ORDER 35. MELASTOMACEÆ.

RHEXIA, L. MEADOW-BEAUTY.

Virginica, L.*

* In North Kingstown I have found this plant with narrow leaves and white flowers.

ORDER 36. **LYTHRACEÆ.**

AMMANIA, Houston.

humilis, Michx.   No. Providence, *Congdon.*

LYTHRUM, L. LOOSESTRIFE.

1. **Hyssopifolia**, L.   Warren, *Greene.*
2. **alatum**, Pursh.   Buttonwoods, *Bailey.*
3. **Salicaria**, L.

NESÆA, Commerson. SWAMP LOOSESTRIFE.

verticillata, H. B. K.

CUPHEA, Jacq.

viscosissima, Jacq.   Tiverton, *Prof. Sargent.*

ORDER 37. **CUCURBITACEÆ.**

SICYOS, L. STAR-CUCUMBER.

angulatus, L.

ECHINOCYSTIS, T. & G. WILD BALSAM-APPLE.

lobatus, T. & G.

ORDER 38. **CACTACEÆ.**

OPUNTIA, Tourn. PRICKLY PEAR.

vulgaris, Mill.   Westerly, *Bennett.*

ORDER 39. **FICOIDEÆ.**

MOLLUGO, L.

verticillata, L. INDIAN CHICK-WEED.

ORDER 40. **UMBELLIFERÆ.**

HYDROCOTYLE, Tourn. WATER PENNYWORT.

1. **Americana**, L.
2. **umbellata**, L.
3. **interrupta**, Muhl.   Block Island, *Olney.*

CRANTZIA, Nutt.

lineata, Nutt.

SANICULA, Tourn. SANICLE, BLACK SNAKEROOT.

1. **Canadensis**, L.
2. **Marilandica**, L.

DAUCUS, Tourn. CARROT.
Carota, L.

HERACLEUM, L. COW-PARSNEP.
lanatum, Michx.

PASTINACA, Tourn. PARSNEP.
sativa, L.

ANGELICA, L.
atropurpurea, L.
Archangelica, Hoffm.

CŒLOPLEURUM, Ledeb.
Gmelini, Ledeb.   Narragansett.
Archangelica, Hoffm.

ÆTHUSA, L. FOOLS' PARSLEY.
Cynapium, L.

LIGUSTICUM, L. LOVAGE.
Scoticum, L.

THASPIUM, Nutt. MEADOW PARSNEP.
1. **aureum,** Nutt.
2. **trifoliatum,** var. **atropurpureum,** T. & G. Warwick,
   Olney.

PIMPINELLA, Benth.
integerrima, Benth & Hook.
Zizia integerrima, D. C.

DISCOPLEURA, D. C. MOCK BISHOP-WEED.
capillacea, D. C.

ÆGAPODIUM, L. GOUT-WEED.
Podagraria, L. Providence, *Bailey.* Wickford, *Bennett.*

CICUTA, L. WATER HEMLOCK.
1. **maculata,** L.
2. **bulbifera,** L.

SIUM, L. WATER-PARSNEP.
1. **cicutæfolium,** Gmel.
   S. lineare, Michx.   N. Kingstown, &c.
2. **Carsoni,** Durand.   No. Kingstown.

CRYPTOTÆNIA, D. C. HONE-WORT.
Canadensis, D. C.

OSMORHIZA, Raf. SWEET CICELY.
1. **longistylis,** D. C.
2. **brevistylis,** D. C.

BIFORA, Hoffm.

radians, M. v. B. Providence, *Bennett.*

CONIUM, L. HEMLOCK.

maculatum, L.

ORDER 41. ARALIACEÆ.

ARALIA, Tourn.

1. racemosa, L. SPIKENARD.
2. hispida, Michx. WILD-ELDER.
3. nudicaulis, L. SARSAPARILLA.
4. quinquefolia, (L.) GINSENG.
5. trifolia, (L.) GINSENG.

ORDER 42. CORNACEÆ.

CORNUS, Tourn. CORNEL.

1. Canadensis, L. DWARF CORNEL.
2. florida, L. FLOWERING DOGWOOD.
3. circinata, L'Her.
4. sericea, L.
5. stolonifera, Michx. *Mr. Hunt.*
6. paniculata, L'Her.
7. alternifolia, L.

NYSSA, L. TUPELO.

multiflora, Wang.

DIVISION II. MONOPETALÆ.

ORDER 43. CAPRIFOLIACEÆ..

SAMBUCUS, Tourn. ELDER.

1. Canadensis, L.
2. racemosa, L.
    S. pubens, Michx.

VIBURNUM, L. ARROW WOOD.

1. lantanoides, Michx. HOBBLE-BUSH.. Cumberland, Burrillville.
2. acerifolium, L. MAPLE-LEAVED ARROW WOOD.
3. dentatum, L. ARROW WOOD.
4. cassinoides, (L.)
    V. nudum, L. var. cassinoides.
5. nudum, L. WITHE ROD.
6. Lentago, L. SHEEPBERRY. SWEET VIBURNUM.

2

TRIOSTEUM, L. Feverwort.
perfoliatum, L.

LINNÆA, Gronov.
borealis, Gronov.   Snagwood Foster, *Bennett.*

DIERVILLA, Tourn. Bush Honeysuckle.
trifida, Moench.

LONICERA, L. Honeysuckle.
1. coerulea, L.
2. oblongifolia, Muhl.   Johnston, *Hunt & Bailey.*
3. sempervirens, Ait.   Johnston, Cranston, *Bennett.*
4. glauca, Hill.

     L. parviflora, Lam.

Order 44. RUBIACEÆ.

HOUSTONIA, L. Innocence, Bluets.
1. coerulea, L.
2. purpurea, L. var. longifolia.*

CEPHALANTHUS, L. Button Bush.
occidentalis, L.

MITCHELLA, L. Partridge-Berry.
repens, L.

GALIUM, L. Bed-straw Cleavers.
1. Aparine, L.   Silver Spring, *Congdon.*
2. pilosum, Ait.
3. circæzans, Michx.
4. lanceolatum, Torr.
5. trifidum, L.
    var. latifolium.
6. asprellum, Michx.
7. triflorum, Michx.
8. v e r u m , L. Greenwich, *Congdon.* Quidnesset, *Bennett.*

Order 45. COMPOSITÆ.

VERNONIA, Schreb. Iron Weed.
Noveboracensis, Willd.

MIKANIA, Willd. Climbing Hemp-Weed.
scandens, L.

---

 * The narrow-leaved form (H. tenuifolia, Nutt) is found on Hope Island.

EUPATORIUM, Tourn. THOROUGHWORT.
1. **purpureum**, L. JOE-PYE WEED.
   var. **maculatum**, Darl.
2. **hyssopifolium**, L.
3. **teucrifolium**, Willd.
4. **rotundifolium**, L.
   var. **ovatum**, Torr.
   E. pubescens, Muhl.
5. **sessilifolium**, L.
6. **perfoliatum**, L.
7. **ageratoides**, L. f. WHITE SNAKE ROOT.
8. **aromaticum**, L. Quidnessett, *Bennett.* Smithfield, *Congdon.*

    LIATRIS, Schreb. BLAZING STAR.
scariosa, Willd.

    CHRYSOPSIS, Nutt. GOLDEN ASTER.
falcata, Ell.

    SOLIDAGO, L. GOLDEN ROD.
1. **cæsia**, L.
2. **latifolia**, L.
3. **bicolor**, L.
   var. **concolor**, Torr. & Gray. Quidnessett, *Bennett.*
4. **uliginosa**, Nutt.   Hopkinton, &c., *Bennett.*
   S. stricta, Ait.
5. **puberula**, Nutt.
6. **odora**, Ait.
7. **speciosa**, Nutt.   Smithfield, &c.
8. **rugosa**, Mill.
   S. altissima, L.
9. **ulmifolia**, Muhl.
10. **Elliottii**, T. & G.
   S. elliptica, Ait.
11. **neglecta**, T. & G.
   var. **linoides**, T. & G.
   S. linoides. Solander.
12. **arguta**, Ait.
   S. Muhlenbergii, T. & G.
13. **juncea**, Ait.
   S. arguta, Ait, var. juncea.
14. **serotina**, Ait.
   var. **gigantea**, Gray.
   S. gigantea. Ait.
15. **Canadensis**, L.
16. **nemoralis**, Ait.
17. **rigida**, L.   Buttonwood; Quidnessett, *Bennett.*
18. **lanceolata** L.   Quidnessett, &c.
19. **tenuifolia**, Pursh.

SERICOCARPUS, Nees. WHITE-TOPPED ASTER.

1. **solidagineus**, Nees.
2. **conyzoides**, Nees.

ASTER, L. STARWORT, ASTER.

1. **corymbosus**, Ait.
2. **macrophyllus**, L.
3. **Herveyi**, Gray. Tiverton, *Prof. Sargent.*
4. **spectabilis**, Ait.
5. **radula**, Ait. E. Providence. Warwick. Worden's Pond.
6. **Novæ-Angliæ**, L. MICHÆLMAS DAISY.
   var. **rosea**. D. C.
   var.   with rays white! Pettaconsett.
7. **concolor**, L. Near Worden's pond, *Miss Barstow.*
8. **patens**, Ait.
   var. **phlogifolius**, Nees.
9. **undulatus**, L.
10. **cordifolius**, L.
11. **sagittifolius**, Willd.
12. **lævis**, L.
   var. **cyaneus**.
13. **ericoides**, L. No. Providence, *Olney.* E. Greenwich, *Bennett.*
14. **amethystinus**, Nutt. Cumberland, *Congdon.* N. Providence, *Bennett.*
15. **multiflorus**, Ait.
16. **dumosus**, L.
17. **vimineus**, Lam.
   A. miser, L. Ait.
   var. **foliolosus**, Gray.
18. **diffusus**, Ait.
   A. miser, L. Ait., in part.
19. **Tradescanti**, L.
20. **paniculatus**, Lam.
   A. simplex, Willd.
21. **salicifolius**, Ait.
   A. carneus, Nees.
22. **junceus**, Ait.
   A. æsticus, Ait.
23. **longifolius**, Lam.
24. **Novi-Belgii**, L.
   var. **elodes**, Gray.
   A. longifolius, in part.
25. **puniceus**, L.
   var. **lucidulus**.
   A. puniceus, L. var. vimineus.
   var. **lævicaulis**.
26. **umbellatus**, Mill.
   Diplopappus umbellatus, T. & G.

27. **infirmus**, Michx.   S. Kingstown, *Hunt & Bennett.*
     Diplopappus cornifolius, Darl.
28. **linariifolius**, L.
     Diplopappus linariifolius, Hook.
29. **acuminatus**, Michx.
30. **nemoralis**, Ait. Burrillville, *Dr. Robbins.* W. Greenwich, &c.
31. **tenuifolius**, L.
     A. flexuosus, Nutt.
32. **subulatus**, Michx.
     A. linifolius, L.

ERIGERON, L. FLEABANE.

1. **bellidifolius**, Muhl. ROBINS PLANTAIN.
2. **Philadelphicus**, L.
3. **annuus**, Pers.
4. **strigosus**, Muhl.
     var. **discoideus**, Robbins.   Providence, &c.
5. **Canadensis**, L. HORSE WEED, MARES-TAIL.

PLUCHEA, Cass. SALT MARSH FLEABANE.
camphorata, D. C.

ANTENNARIA, R. Br. EVERLASTING.
plantaginifolia, Hook.

' ANAPHALIS, D. C. PEARLY EVERLASTING.
margaritacea, Benth & Hook.
     Antennaria margaritacea, R. Br.

GNAPHALIUM, L.

1. **decurrens**, Ives. EVERLASTING.
2. **polycephalum**, Michx. COMMON EVERLASTING.
3. **uliginosum**, L. LOW CUDWEED.
4. **purpureum**, L. PURPLE CUDWEED.

INULA, L. ELECAMPANE.
Helenium, L.

IVA, L. HIGH WATER SHRUB.
frutescens, L.

AMBROSIA, Tourn. RAGWEED.
artemisiæfolia, L. HORSE WORMWEED.

XANTHIUM, Tourn. COCKLEBUR, CLOTBUR.

1. **strumarium**, L.
2. **Canadense**, Mill. var. **echinatum**.
     X. strumarium, var. echinatum.

3. spinosum, L.   Newport.

RUDBECKIA, L. CONE-FLOWER.

1. laciniata, L.
2. hirta, L. DUTCH-DAISY.

HELIANTHUS, L. SUNFLOWER.

1. divaricatus, L.
2. strumosus, L.
3. decapetalus, L.
4. tuberosus, L. JERUSALEM ARTICHOKE.

COREOPSIS, L. TICKSEED.

1. rosea, Nutt.   Providence, North Providence.
2. trichosperma, Michx.   South Kingstown.
3. discoidea, T. & G.   Quidnesset, *Bennett.*

BIDENS, L.

1. frondosa, L. BEGGAR-TICKS.
2. connata, Muhl. SWAMP BEGGAR-TICKS.
3. cernua, L. SMALL BURMARIGOLD.
4. chrysanthemoides, Michx. LARGE BURMARIGOLD.
5. bipinnata. SPANISH NEEDLES. Cove lands, Providence, *Congdon.*
6. Beckii, Torr. WATER MARIGOLD.

GALINSOGA, Ruiz & Pavon.

parviflora, Cav.   Providence, *Prof. Bailey.*

HELENIUM, L.

1. autumnale, L. SNEEZE-WEED.   Molasses Hill, *Bennett.*
 . nudiflorum, Nutt.   Quinsnaket.
        Leptopoda brachypoda, T. & G.

ANTHEMIS, L.

1. Cotula, L. MAY-WEED.
        Maruta Cotula, D. C.
2. arvensis, L. CORN CHAMOMILE.
3. nobilis, L. CHAMOMILE. Fully established!

ACHILLEA, L. YARROW.

Millefolium, L.*

CHRYSANTHEMUM, L. WHITE WEED.

1. Leucanthemum, L. OX-EYE DAISY.
        Leucanthemum vulgare, Lam.
2. Parthenium, Pers. FEVER FEW.
        Leucanthemum Parthenium, Godron.

* A variety with very rosy flowers grows on Wakefield Hill, Warwick.

3. **Balsamita**, L., var. **tanacetoides**, Boiss. Balm. Established!

TANACETUM, L. Tansy.

vulgare, L.
      var. **crispum.** Quidnessett.

ARTEMISIA, L. Wormwood.

1. **caudata**, Michx.
2. **vulgaris**, L. Mugwort.
3. **Absinthium**, L. Wormwood.
4. **biennis**, L.   Providence, *Prof. Bailey.*

TUSSILAGO, Tourn. Colts Foot.

Farfara, L.   Smithfield, Cranston, *Bennett.*

SENECIO, L. Groundsel.

1. **aureus**, L. Squaw-Weed.
      var. **oboyatus**, T. & G.
      var. **Balsamitæ**, T. & G.
2. **vulgaris**, L.
3. **viscosus**, L.   Providence, &c.

CACALIA, L. Indian Plantain.

suaveolens, L.   Providence, &c. Not common.

ERECHTHITES, Raf. Fire-Weed.

hieracifolia, Raf.

ARCTIUM, L. Burdock.

Lappa, L.
      Lappa officinalis, Allioni.
      var. **majus.**
      var. **minus.** Wanskuck; Burrillville. *Dr. Robbins.*

CNICUS, L. (*Tourn.*) Thistle.

1. **arvensis**, Hoffm. Canada Thistle.
      Cirsium arvense, Scop.
2. **lanceolatus**, Hoffm.
      Cirsium lanceolatum, Scop.
3. **horridulus**, Pursh. Yellow Thistle.
      Cirsium horridulum, Michx.
4. **pumilus**, Torr. Pasture Thistle.
      Corsium pumilum, Spreng.
5. **altissimus**, Willd.
      Cirsium altissimum, Spreng.
      var. **discolor.**
      Cirsium discolor, Gray.
6. **muticus**, Pursh. Swamp Thistle.
      Cirsium muticum, Michx.

ONOPORDON, Vaill. CATEEN THISTLE.
Acanthium, L.

CENTAUREA, L.

1. Cyanus, L. CORN FLOWER.
2. nigra, K. KNAP-WEED.
3. Jacea, L.   Providence, *Bennett*.

LAMPSANA, Tourn. NIPPLE-WORT.
communis, L.

KRIGIA, Schreb. DWARF DANDELION.
Virginica, L.

CICHORIUM, Tourn. CHICORY.
Intybus, L.

LEONTODON, L. FALL DANDELION.
autumnalis, L.

HIERACIUM, Tourn. HAWKWEED.

1. aurantiacum, L.   Providence, &c.
2. Canadense, Michx.
3. paniculatum, L.
4. venosum, L RATTLESNAKE-WEED.
5. marianum, Willd.
            H. scabrum, Michx, in part.
6. scabrum, Michx.
7. Gronovii, L.

PRENANTHES, Vaill. RATTLESNAKE-ROOT.

1. alba, L. WHITE LETTUCE.
            Nabalus alba, Hook.
2. Serpentaria, Pursh. LION'S FOOT.
            Nabalus Fraseri, D. C.
3. altissima, L.
            Nabalus altissimus, Hook.

TARAXACUM, Haller. DANDELION.
officinale, Weber.
            T. Dens-leonis, Desf.

LACTUCA, Tourn. LETTUCE.

1. Canadensis, L.
2. integrifolia, Bigelow.
            L. Canadensis, T. & G. var.
3. hirsuta, Muhl.
            L. Canadensis, var. sanguinea, T. & G.

4. leucophæa, Gray.
>   *Mulgedium leucophœum, D. C.*

> **SONCHUS, L.** Sow Thistle.

1. oleraceus, L.
2. asper, Vill.
3. arvensis, L.

> ORDER 46. **LOBELIACEÆ.**

> **LOBELIA, L.**

1. cardinalis, L. Cardinal Flower.
>   var. alba.
2. inflata, L. Indian Tobacco.
3. spicata, Lam.
4. Dortmanna, L. Water Lobelia.

> ORDER 47. **CAMPANULACEÆ.**

> **CAMPANULA, Tourn.** Bellwort.

1. aparinoides, Pursh.
2. rapunculoides, L.

> **SPECULARIA, Heister.** Venus Looking-Glass.
> perfoliata, A. D. C.

> ORDER 48. **ERICACEÆ,**

> **GAYLUSSACIA, H. B. K.** Huckleberry.

1. dumosa, T. & G. S. Kingstown. *Mr. Hunt.* Quidnessett,
>   *Bennett.*
2. frondosa, T. & G. Dangleberry.
3. resinosa, T. & G. Black Huckleberry.

> **VACCINIUM, L.**

1. Oxycoccus, L. Small Cranberry.
2. macrocarpon, Ait. Large Cranberry.
3. Pennsylvanicum, Lam.* Low Blueberry.
4. vacillans, Solander.* Canada Blueberry.
5. corymbosum, L.* Swamp Whortleberry.
>   var. amœnum,
>   var. glabrum.
>   var. atrococcum.

> **CHIOGENES, Salisb.** Snowberry.
> hispidula, T. & G. Foster, &c. Rare.

> **ARCTOSTAPHYLOS, Adans.** Bearberry.
> Uva-Ursi, Spreng.

* These species produce sometimes the (so-called) white whortleberries.

EPIGÆA, L.

repens, L. MAYFLOWER, TRAILING ARBUTUS.

GAULTHERIA, Kalm.

procumbens, L. WINTERGREEN.

LEUCOTHOE, Don.

racemosa, Gray.

CASSANDRA, Don. LEATHERLEAF.

calyculata, Don.

ANDROMEDA, L.

1. **Mariana**, L. STAGGER-BUSH.
2. **ligustrina**, Muhl.

CLETHRA, L.

alnifolia, L. SWEET PEPPER.

KALMIA, L. LAUREL.

1. **latifolia**. L. CALICO-BUSH, High Laurel.
2. **angustifolia**, L. LAMB-KILL, Low Laurel.

RHODODENDRON, L.

1. **viscosum**, Torr. WHITE SWAMP-CHEESE.
   Azalea viscosa, L.
2. **nudiflorum**, Torr. PINK AZALEA.
   Azalea nudiflora, L.
3. **maximum**, L. ROSE-BAY.   S. Kingstown, &c.
4. **Rhodora**, (L.)
   Rhodora Canadensis, L.

PYROLA, Tourn.

1. **rotundifolia**, L. WOOD-LETTUCE.
2. **elliptica**, Nutt. SHIN-LEAF.
3. **chlorantha**, Swartz. Somewhat rare.
4. **secunda**, L.

MONESES, Salisb.

uniflora, Salisb. Burrillville, *Bennett.* Smithfield, *Mr. Russell.*

CHIMAPHILA, Pursh.

1. **umbellata**, Nutt. PRINCE'S PINE, PIPSISSEWA.
2. **maculata**, Pursh. SPOTTED PIPSISSEWA.

MONOTROPA, L.

1. **uniflora**, L. INDIAN PIPES.
2. **Hypopitys**, L. PINE-SAP.

ORDER 49. **AQUIFOLIACEÆ.**

ILEX, L.

1. **opaca,** Ait. HOLLY.   So. Kingstown, &c.
2. **verticillata,** Gray. BLACK ALDER.
3. **lævigata,** Gray. SMOOTH ALDER.
4. **glabra,** Gray, INKBERRY.   N. Kingstown.

NEMOPANTHES, Raf.

Canadensis, D. C. MOUNTAIN HOLLY.

ORDER 50. **EBENACEÆ.**

DISPYROS, L.

Virginiana, L. PERSIMMON.   Woonsocket, *Olney.*

ORDER 51. **PLANTAGINACEÆ.**

PLANTAGO, L. PLANTAIN.

1. **major,** L.
2. **Rugelii,** Decaisne.   E. Providence, *Bennett.*
        P. Kamschatica, Cham.
3. **decipiens,** Barneoud.
        P. maritima, L. var. juncoides.
4. **lanceolata,** L. RIBWORT.
5. **Virginica,** L.   Providence.
6. **pusilla,** Nutt.   Potawomut, *Congdon.*
7. **Patagonica,** Jacq., var. **aristata,** Gray. Quidnessett,
    Bennett.

ORDER 52. **PLUMBAGINACEÆ.**

STATICE, Tourn. MARSH ROSEMARY.

Limonium, L., var. **Caroliniana.**

ORDER 53. **PRIMULACEÆ.**

TRIENTALIS, L. CHICKWEED-WINTERGREEN.

Americana, Pursh.

LYSIMACHIA, Tourn. LOOSESTRIFE.

1. **stricta,** Ait.
2. **quadrifolia,** L.
3. **thyrsiflora,** L.   *Dr. Geo. Thurber.*
4. **nummularia,** L.
5. **vulgaris,** L.   Middletown, *Prof. Bailey.*

STEIRONEMA, Raf. LOOSESTRIFE.

1. **ciliatum,** Raf.
      Lysimachia ciliata, L.

2. **lanceolatum,** Gray.
>>> *Lysimachia lanceolata, Walt.*
>>> var. **hybridum.**
>>> *Lysimachia lanceolata, var.*

ANAGALLIS, Tourn. PIMPERNEL.
arvensis, L.

SAMOLUS, L. WATER PIMPERNEL.
Valerandi, L., var. **Americanus,** Gray.

HOTTONIA, L. FEATHERFOIL.
inflata, Ell.   Little Compton, &c.

ORDER 54. **LENTIBULACEÆ.**

UTRICULARIA, L. BLADDERWORT.
1. **inflata,** L.
2. **macrorhiza,** Le Conte.
>>> *U. vulgaris, L.*
3. **minor,** L.   Smithfield, *Congdon.*
4. **clandestina,** L.   East Providence; Quidnessett.
5. **intermedia,** Hayne.   Providence.
6. **biflora,** Lam.   *J. W. Congdon, Esq.*
7. **gibba,** L.
8. **purpurea,** Walt.   Lincoln. Cranston, *Congdon.*
9. **resupinata,** Greene.   S. Kingstown, *Olney.*
10. **cornuta,** Michx.
11. **subulata,** L.   Worden's Pond, *Congdon.*

ORDER 55. **OROBANCHACEÆ.**

EPIPHEGUS, Nutt. BEECH-DROPS.
Virginiana, Barton.

CONOPHOLIS, Wallroth. CANCER-ROOT.
Americana, Wallr.   *Olney.*

APHYLLON, Mitchell.
uniflorum, T. & G. BROOM-RAPE.

ORDER 56. **SCROPHULARIACEÆ.**

VERBASCUM, L. MULLEIN.
1. **Thapsus,** L.
2. **Blattaria,** L.* MOTH-MULLEIN.
3. **Lychnitis,** L. WHITE-MULLEIN.

* The yellow flowered form is seldom found with us.

LINARIA, Tourn. Toad-Flax.
1. **Canadensis**, Spreng.
2. **vulgaris**, Mill. Butter and Eggs.
3. **Elatine**, Mill.   Middletown, *Bennett.*

SCROPHULARIA, Tourn. Figwort.
nodosa, L.

CHELONE, Tourn. Snake-Head.
glabra, L.

PENTSTEMON, Mitchell.
pubescens, Solander.   Cranston, *Bennett;* Conanicut, *L. W. Russell.*

MIMULUS, L. Monkey-Flower.
1. **ringens**, L.
2. **alatus**, Ait.

GRATIOLA, L. Hedge-Hyssop.
1. **Virginiana**, L.
2. **aurea**, Muhl.

ILYSANTHES, Raf. False Pimpernel.
gratioloides, Benth.

LIMOSELLA, L. Mudwort.
aquatica, L., var. tenuifolia, Hoffm.   Point Judith.

VERONICA, L. Speedwell.
1. **Virginica**, L. Culver's Root.   West boundary of State.
2. **Anagallis**, L.
3. **Americana**, Schweinitz.
4. scutellata, L.
5. officinalis, L.   Providence, *J. L. B.*
6. serpyllifolia, L.
7. peregrina, L.
8. **arvensis**, L.
9. **agrestis**, L.   Providence, Apponaug.
10. **hederæfolia**, L.   (In Herb. *Olney.*)

GERARDIA, L. False Foxglove.
1. **purpurea**, L.*
2. **maritima**, Raf.*
3. **tenuifolia**, Vahl.*
4. flava, L.
5. quercifolia, Pursh.
6. pedicularia, L.

* The flowers of these species are frequently white!

CASTILLEIA, Mutis. PAINTED CUP.
coccinea, Spreng.

PEDICULARIS, Tourn. BETONY.
1. Canadensis, L.
2. lanceolata, Michx.   Exeter, *Prof. Bailey.*

MELAMPYRUM, Tourn. COW WHEAT.
Americanum, Michx.

ORDER 57. **VERBENACEÆ.**

VERBENA, L.
1. hastata. L.
2. urticifolia, L.
3. officinalis, L.   Cranston, *Bennett.*

PHRYMA, L.
Leptostachya, L.

ORDER 58. **LABIATÆ.**

TEUCRIUM, L. GERMANDER.
Canadense, L.

TRICHOSTEMA, L. BLUE CURLS.
1. dichotomum, L.*
2. lineare, Nutt.   N. Providence.

MENTHA. L. MINT.
1. viridis, L. SPEARMINT.
2. piperita, L. PEPPERMINT.
3. Canadensis, L. CANADA-MINT.

LYCOPUS, L. HOARHOUND.
1. Virginicus, L. BUGLE WEED.
2. sinuatus, Ell.
         L. Europæus L. var.
3. lucidus, Ell.   Spectacle Pond, *Congdon.*
         L. Europæus L. var.

PYCNANTHEMUM, Michx. BASIL.
1. incanum, Michx.
2. muticum, Pers.
3. lanceolatum, Pursh.
4. linifolium, Pursh.

THYMUS, L. THYME.
Serpyllum, L.   Matunuck, *Bennett.*

* A variety with pale pink flowers occurs at Quidnessett.

CALAMINTHA, Moench. CALAMINT.
Clinopodium, Benth.

HEDEOMA, Pers. PENNYROYAL.
pulegioides, Pers.

COLLINSONIA, L. HORSE-BALM.
Canadensis, L.

MONARDA, L. HORSE MINT.
fistulosa, L., var. mollis.   Westerly, &c.

NEPETA, L.
1. **Cataria,** L. CATNEP.
2. **Glechoma,** Benth. GILL, GROUND IVY.

PHYSOSTEGIA, Benth. DRAGON-HEAD.
Virginiana, Benth.   E. Providence, *Mr. Leland.*

BRUNELLA, Tourn. SELF-HEAL.
vulgaris, L.

SCUTELLARIA, L. SCULL-CAP.
1. integrifolia, L.   Found once in Cranston.
2. galericulata, L.
3. lateriflora, L.

MARRUBIUM, L. HOREHOUND.
vulgare, L.   East Greenwich, &c.

GALEOPSIS, L. HEMP-NETTLE.
1. **Tetrahit,** L.
2. **Ladanum,** L.

STACHYS, L. HEDGE-NETTLE.
1. palustris, L.
2. aspera, Michx.
              S. palustris L. var.
3. cordata, Riddell.   N. Kingstown, &c.
              S. palustris L. var.
4. hyssopifolia, Michx.   Smithfield, *Congdon.*

LEONURUS, L. MOTHERWORT.
Cardiaca, L.

LAMIUM, L. DEAD-NETTLE.
1. amplexicaule, L.
2. purpureum, L.

3. **album**, L.

        BALLOTA, L. HOREHOUND.

nigra, L.   Providence, Westerly; rather rare.

ORDER 59. **BORRAGINACEÆ.**

        ECHIUM, Tourn. VIPER'S BUGLOSS.

vulgare, L.   Providence.

        LYCOPSIS, L. BUGLOSS.

arvensis, L.   Providence, &c.

        SYMPHTUM, Tourn. COMFREY.

officinale, L.

    ONOSMODIUM, Michx. FALSE GROMWELL.

Virginianum, D. C.   Near Greenville, &c.

    LITHOSPERMUM, Tourn. GROMWELL.

1. **arvense**, L. CORN-GROMWELL.
2. **officinale**, L.   Uncommon.

        MYOSOTIS, L. FORGET-ME-NOT.

1. **palustris**, With.
2. **laxa**, Lehm.
               M. palustris, rar. laxa.
3. **arvensis**, Hoffm.
4. **verna**, Nutt.

    CYNOGLOSSUM, Tourn. HOUND'S TONGUE.

1. **officinale**, L.   East Greenwich, &c.

    ECHINOSPERMUM, Swartz. STICK-SEED.

Virginicum, Lehm.
         Cynoglossum Morisoni, D. C.

ORDER 60. **CONVOLVULACEÆ.**

        IPOMÆA, L.

purpurea, Lam. MORNING-GLORY.

    CONVOLVULUS, L. BIND-WEED.

1. **arvensis**, L.
2. **sepium**, L.
         Calystegia sepium, R. Br.
3. **spithamæa**, (Pursh.)
         Calystegia spithamæa.

CUSCUTA. DODDER.

1. **inflexa**, Engelm.   Spectacle Pond, *in herb. Olney.*
2. **chlorocarpa**, Engelm.
3. **Gronovii**, Willd.
4. **compacta**, Juss. East Greenwich, *Congdon;* Quidnessett, *Bennett.*

ORDER 61. SOLANACEÆ.

SOLANUM, Tourn.

1. **Dulcamara**, L. BITTERSWEET.
2. **nigrum**, L. NIGHTSHADE.
3. **rostratum**, Dunal.   East Providence, *Bennett.*

PHYSALIS, L. GROUND CHERRY.

1. **Virginiana**, Mill.
2. **angulata**, L.   Providence, &c.
3. **pubescens**, L.   Providence.
4. **viscosa**, L.   Coventry, near Connecticut line, *Bennett.*
5. **Alkekengi**, L. STRAWBERRY TOMATO.   Escaped.
6. **Peruviana**, L.   Providence, *Prof. Bailey.*

NICANDRA, Adans.

physaloides, Gaertn. APPLE OF PERU.

LYCIUM, L.

vulgare, Dunal. MATRIMONY VINE.

HYOSCYAMUS, Tourn. HENBANE.

niger, L.   Block Island, *Olney.*

DATURA, L. THORN APPLE.

1. **Stramonium**, L.
2. **Tatula**, L.

ORDER 62. GENTIANACEÆ.

SABBATIA, Adans.

1. **chloroides**, Pursh.
2. **stellaris**, Pursh.   Narragansett, *Mr. Hunt.* Matunuck.

GENTIANA, L. GENTIAN.

1. **crinita**, Froelich. FRINGED GENTIAN.
2. **Andrewsii**, Griseb. BOX GENTIAN.

BARTONIA, Muhl.

tenella, Muhl.

MENYANTHES, Tourn. BUCK-BEAN.

trifoliata, L.

3

LIMNANTHEMUM, Gmelin.
lacunosum, Griseb. FLOATING HEARTS.

ORDER 63. **APOCYNACEÆ**..

APOCYNUM, Tourn. DOGBANE, INDIAN HEMP.
1. androsæmifolium, L.
2. cannabinum, L., & vars.

ORDER 64. **ASCLEPIADACEÆ**.

ASCLEPIAS, L. MILK-WEED
1. Cornuti, Decaisne.
2. phytolaccoides, Pursh.
3. purpurascens, L.
4. quadrifolia, Jacq.   Not common.
5. incarnata, L.
    var. pulchra.
6. obtusifolia, Michx.
7. tuberosa, L. PLEURISY-ROOT, BUTTERFLY-WEED.
8. verticillata, L.

ORDER 65. **OLEACEÆ**.

LIGUSTRUM, Tourn. PRIVET.
vulgare, L.

FRAXINUS, Tourn. ASH.
1. Americana, L. WHITE ASH.
2. pubescens, Lam. RED ASH.
3. viridis, Mich. f.   Nooseneck.
4. sambucifolia, Lam. WATER ASH, BLACK ASH.

DIVISION III. APETALÆ.

ORDER 66. **PHYTOLACCACEÆ**.

PHYTOLACCA, Tourn. POKE, GARGET.
decandra, L.

ORDER 67. **CHENOPODIACEÆ**.

CHENOPODIUM, L. GOOSEFOOT.
1. album, L. PIG-WEED.
    var. viride.
2. glaucum, L.

3. **urbicum**, L.
>   var. **rhombifolium.**
4. **murale**, L.
5. **hybridum**, L.
6. **Botrys.** Jerusalem Oak.
7. **ambrosioides**, L., var. **anthelminticum.** Worm-
>   seed.

BLITUM, Tourn. Blite.
maritimum, Nutt.   Quidnessett, Block Island.

ATRIPLEX, Tourn. Orache.
1. **patula**, L.
2. **arenaria**, Nutt.   Quidnessett, Newport.

SALICORNIA, Tourn. Glasswort, Samphire.
1. **herbacea**, L.
2. **Virginica**, L.
3. **fruticosa**, L., var. **ambigua.**

SUÆDA, Forskal. Sea Blite.
maritima, Dumortier.

SALSOLA, L. Saltwort.
Kali, L.

Order 68. PARONYCHIEÆ.

ANYCHIA, Michx. Forked Chickweed.
dichotoma, Michx.

SCLERANTHUS, L. Knawel.
annuus, L.

Order 69. AMARANTACEÆ.

AMARANTUS, Tourn. Amaranth.
1. **hypochondriacus**, L. Love-lies-bleeding.
2. **paniculatus**, L.
3. **hybridus**, L.
>   *A. retroflexus, L. var.*
4. **albus**, L.
5. **pumilus**, Raf.   Easton's Beach, *Bennett.*
6. **spinosus**, L. Thorny Amaranth.   *Congdon.*

ACNIDA, L. Water Hemp.
cannabina, L.

ORDER 70. **POLYGONACEÆ.**

POLYGONUM, L. Knotweed.

    orientale, L. Prince's Feather.
2. **Careyi**, Olney.
3. **Hartwrightii**, Gray.   Providence.
4. **incarnatum**, Ell.   Apponaug, &c.
5. **Persicaria**, L. Lady's Thumb.
6. **Hydropiper**, L. Smartweed.
7. **acre**, H. B. K. Water Smartweed.
8. **hydropiperoides**, Michx. Water-Pepper.
9. **amphibium**, L.
10. **Muhlenbergii**, Watson.
           P. amphibium, var. terrestre.
11. **Virginianum**, L.
12. **articulatum**, L. Joint-Weed.
13. **aviculare**, L. Knot-Grass.
14. **erectum**, L.
           P. aviculare, var.
15. **maritimum**, L.   Newport, &c.
16. **ramosissimum**.   Barrington. *Olney.* Newport, &c.
17. **tenue**, L.
18. **arifolium**, L. Tear-Thumb.
19. **sagittatum**, L. Tear-Thumb.
20. **Convolvulus**, L. Black Bindweed
21. **cilinode**, Michx.   Johnston, *Bennett.*
22. **dumetorum**, L. Climbing False Buckwheat.

FAGOPYRUM, Tourn. Buckwheat.
    esculentum, Moench.

RUMEX, L. Dock.

1. **salicifolius**, Weinm.   Providence ; banks of Seekonk.
2. **verticillatus**, L.   Point Judith, &c.
3. **maritimus**, L.   Newport, &c.
4. **crispus**, L. Narrow Dock.
5. **obtusifolius**. L.
6. **Acetosella**, L. Sorrel.

ORDER 71. **LAURACEÆ.**

SASSAFRAS, Nees.
officinale, Nees. Sassafras.

LINDERA, Thunberg.
Benzoin, Meisner. Fever-Bush, Spice-Bush.

ORDER 72. **THYMELEACEÆ.**

DIRCA, L. LEATHERWOOD.
palustris, L.   Cumberland, *Olney;* Burrillville, &c.

ORDER 73. **SANTALACEÆ.**

COMANDRA, Nutt. BASTARD TOAD FLAX.
umbellata, Nutt.

ORDER 74. **CERATOPHYLLACEÆ.**

CERATOPHYLLUM, L. HORNWORT.
demersum, L., var. **commune.**   Stillwater.
                var. **echinatum.**   Wenscott Reservoir.

ORDER 75. **PODOSTEMACEÆ.**

PODOSTEMON, Michx. RIVER WEED.
ceratophyllus, Michx.

ORDER 76. **EUPHORBIACEÆ.**

EUPHORBIA, L. SPURGE.
1. polygonifolia, L.
2. maculata, L.
3. hypericifolia, L.
4. **Cyparissias**, L. CYPRESS.
5. **Peplus**, L.   Newport. *Congdon;* Matunuck, *Bennett.*

    ACALYPHA, L. THREE-SEEDED MERCURY.
    Virginica, L.
                var. **gracilens.**

ORDER 77. **URTICACEÆ.**

ULMUS, L. ELM.
1. fulva, Michx. SLIPPERY ELM.   East Providence. &c.
2. **Americana**, L.

    CELTIS, Tourn. HACKBERRY.
    occidentalis, L., & vars.

    URTICA, Tourn. NETTLE.
1. gracilis, Ait.
2. **dioica**, L.
3. **urens**, L.

LAPORTEA, Gaudichaud. WOOD NETTLE.
Canadensis, Gaud.

PILEA, Lindl. CLEARWEED.
pumila, Gray.

BOEHMERIA, Jacq. FALSE NETTLE.
cylindrica, Willd.

PARIETARIA, Tourn. PELLITORY.
Pennsylvanica, Muhl.

CANNABIS, Tourn. HEMP.
sativa, L.

HUMULUS, L. HOP.
Lupulus, L.

ORDER 78. **PLATANACEÆ.**

PLATANUS, L. PLANE.
occidentalis, L. BUTTONBALL, SYCAMORE.

ORDER 79. **JUGLANDACEÆ.**

JUGLANS, L. WALNUT.
1. cinerea, L. BUTTERNUT.
2. nigra, L. BLACK WALNUT.   Doubtfully native?

CARYA, Nutt. HICKORY.
1. alba, Nutt. WHITE WALNUT, SHAGBARK.
2. microcarpa, Nutt.   Providence, &c.
3. sulcata, Nutt. SHELL-BARK.   *J. W. Congdon, Esq.*
4. tomentosa, Nutt. MOCKER-NUT.
5. porcina, Nutt, & vars. PIG-NUT.
6. amara, Nutt. BITTER-NUT.

ORDER 80. **CUPULIFERÆ.**

QUERCUS, L. OAK.
1. alba, L. WHITE OAK.
2. obtusiloba, Michx. POST OAK.   Quidnessett, *Bennett.*
3. bicolor, Willd. SWAMP WHITE OAK.
4. Prinus, L.* CHESTNUT OAK.   Providence!
     var. monticola.   Smithfield, &c.
     var. humilis. CHINQUAPIN OAK.
5. ilicifolia, Wang. BEAR OAK.

*Q. macrocarpa, Mx., is reported from Buck Hill Woods.

6. **coccinea**, Wang. SCARLET OAK.
    var. **tinctoria.** YELLOW BARK.
    var. **ambigua.** GRAY OAK. East Providence, &c.
7. **rubra**, L. RED OAK.
    var. **runcinata.**   E. Providence, S. Kingstown.
8. **palustris**, Du Roi. PIN OAK. Cumberland, *Mr. Hunt ;* S.
  Kingstown, &c.

CASTANEA, Tourn. CHESTNUT.
vesca, L., var. **Americana**, Michx.

FAGUS, Tourn. BEECH.
ferruginea, Ait.

CORYLUS, Tourn. HAZEL.
1. **Americana**, Walt.
2. **rostrata**, Ait.

OSTRYA, Micheli. HOP HORN-BEAM.
Virginica, Willd.

CARPINUS, L. IRON WOOD.
Americana, Michx.

ORDER 81. **MYRICACEÆ.**
MYRICA, L.
1. **Gale**, L. SWEET GALE.
2. **cerifera**, L. BAYBERRY.
3. **Comptonia**, C. DC. SWEET-FERN.
    Comptonia asplenifolia, Ait.

ORDER 82. **BETULACEÆ.**
BETULA, Tourn. BIRCH.
1. **lenta**, L. CHERRY BIRCH, BLACK BIRCH.
2. **lutea**, Mich. f. YELLOW BIRCH.
3. **alba**, var. **populifolia**, Spach. GRAY BIRCH.
4. **papyracea**, Ait. CANOE BIRCH.   Smithfield, &c.
5. **nigra**, L. RED BIRCH.   Buck Hill Woods.

ALNUS, Tourn. ALDER.
1. **incana**, Willd. HOARY ALDER.
2. **serrulata**, Ait. SMOOTH ALDER.

ORDER 83. **SALICACEÆ.**
POPULUS, Tourn. POPLAR.
1. **tremuloides**, Michx. ASPEN.

2. **grandidentata**, Michx.
3. **monilifera**, Ait.   South Kingstown. Native?
4. **balsamifera**, L., var. **candicans**. BALM OF GILEAD.
5. **alba**, L. WHITE POPLAR.

SALIX, Tourn. WILLOW.

1. **tristis**, Ait. SAGE WILLOW.
2. **humilis**, Marshall.
3. **discolor**, Muhl.
4. **sericea**, Marshall.
5. **petiolaris**, Sm.   Woodlawn.
6. **purpurea**, L.
7. **viminalis**, L.
8. **cordata**, Muhl, & vars.
9. **livida**, Wahl., var. **occidentalis**.
10. **lucida**, Muhl.
11. **nigra**, Marshall.
        var. **falcata**.   Providence.
        var. **amygdaloides**.   Neutakonkanut.
12. **fragilis**, L.
13. **alba**, L.
14. **longifolia**, Muhl.
15. **myrtilloides**, L.   Johnston, J. W. Congdon.

SUB-CLASS II. GYMNOSPERMÆ.

ORDER 84. CONIFERÆ.

PINUS, Tourn. PINE.

1. **rigida**, Miller. PITCH PINE.
2. **resinosa**, Ait.
3. **Strobus**, L. WHITE PINE.

PICEA, Lk. SPRUCE.

nigra, Lk. BLACK SPRUCE.   Johnston, Foster, &c.
                Abies nigra, Peir.

TSUGA, Caw. HEMLOCK SPRUCE.

Canadensis, (Endl), Carriere.
                Abies Canadensis, Michx.

LARIX, Tourn. LARCH, HACKMATACK.

Americana. Mx.   West Greenwich. Native!

CHAMÆCYPARIS. WHITE CEDAR.

sphæroidea, Spach.
                Cupressus thyoides, L.

JUNIPERUS, L.
1. **communis**, L. JUNIPER.
2. **Virginiana**, L. RED CEDAR.
3. **Sabina**, L., var. **procumbens**.   E. Providence.

TAXUS, Tourn. YEW.
baccata, L., var. **Canadensis**.   Snagwood, Foster.

CLASS II. MONOCOTYLEDONEÆ.

ORDER 85. ARACEÆ.

ARISÆMA, Martius.
1. **triphyllum**, Torr. INDIAN TURNIP.
2. **Dracontium**, Schott.   Providence, (*Hedge.*)

PELTANDRA, Raf. ARROW ARUM.
Virginica, Raf.

CALLA, L. WATER ARUM.
palustris. L.

SYMPLOCARPUS, Salisb. SKUNK CABBAGE.
fœtidus, Salisb.

ORONTIUM, L. GOLDEN-CLUB.
aquaticum, L.   Local.

ACORUS, L. SWEET FLAG.
Calamus, L.

ORDER 86. LEMNACEÆ.

LEMNA, L. DUCKWEED.
1. **minor**, L.
2. **polyrhiza**, L.   Newport.

ORDER 87. TYPHACEÆ.

TYPHA, Tourn. CAT-TAIL.
1. **latifolia**, L.
2. **angustifolia**, L.

SPARGANIUM, Tourn. BUR-REED.
1. **Eurycarpum**, Engelm.
2. **simplex**, Hudson.

ORDER 88. **NAIADACEÆ.**

NAIAS, L. NAIAD.

flexilis, Rostk.

ZANNICHELLIA, Micheli. HORNED POND-WEED.
palustris, L.

ZOSTERA, L. EEL-GRASS, WRACK.
marina, L.

RUPPIA, L. DITCH-GRASS.
maritima, L.

POTAMOGETON, Tourn. POND-WEED.

1. natans, L.
2. **Oakesianus**, Robbins.   *Olney.*
3. **Claytonii**, Tuckerm.
4. **Vaseyi**, Robbins.   *In herb. Olney.*
5. **hybridus**, Michx., var. ——.   Westerly, &c.
6. **Spirillus**, Tuck.   *Robbins;* Quidnessett, *Bennett.*
7. **lonchites**, Tuck. (?)   So. Kingstown.
8. **gramineus**, L., var. **graminfolius.**
             var. **heterophyllus.**
             var. **myriophyllus.**   Gorton's Pond.
9. **perfoliatus**, L.
10. **compressus**, L.
11. **pauciflorus**, Pursh.   Niantic, &c.
12. **pusillus**, L.
13. **gemmiparus**, Robbins.   Lonsdale, &c.
14. **pectinatus**, L.
15. **Robbinsii**, Oakes.   Smithfield.
16. **Tuckermani**, Robbins.

(Our Potamogetons were kindly revised by Dr. Robbins a short
time only before his death; his last botanical work.)

ORDER 89. **ALISMACEÆ.**

TRIGLOCHIN, L. ARROW GRASS.

1. palustre, L.
2. maritimum, L.

SCHEUCHZERIA, L.
palustris, L.   N. Providence, *Olney.*

ALISMA, L. WATER PLANTAIN.
Plantago, L., var. **Americanum.**

SAGITTARIA, L. Arrow-Head.

1. variabilis, Engelm, var. obtusa.
   var. latifolia.
   var. hastata.
   var. diversifolia.
   var. angustifolia.
   var. gracilis.
2. calycina, Engelm.   Woonasquatucket, &c.
3. graminea, Michx.   Benedict's Pond, &c.
4. heterophylla, Pursh.   *Olney.*

Order 90. **HYDROCHARIDACEÆ.**

ANACHARIS, Richard. Water-Weed.
Canadensis, Planchon.

VALLISNERIA, Micheli. Tape Grass, Water Celery.
spiralis, L.   Barrington, &c.

Order 91. **ORCHIDACEÆ.**

ORCHIS, L. Orchis.
spectabilis, L.   Scituate, *Flint.*

HABENARIA, R. Br. Orchis.

1. tridentata, Hook.
2. virescens, Spreng.
3. viridis. R. Br., var. bracteata, Reich.   Lime Rock.
4. Hookeri, Torr.   *Hunt, Flint.*
5. ciliaris, R. Br. Yellow Fringed Orchis.
6. blephariglottis, Hook. White Fringed Orchis.
   var. holopetala. *Hedge;* Quidnessett,
              Bennett.
7. lacera, R. Br. Ragged Fringed Orchis.
8. psycodes, Gray. Small Purple Orchis.
9. fimbriata, R. Br. Large Purple Orchis. So. Kingstown.

GOODYERA, R. Br. Rattlesnake Plantain.

1. repens, R. Br.   Smithfield; rare.
2. pubescens, R. Br.

SPIRANTHES, Richard. Ladies' Tresses.

1. cernua, Richard.
2. graminea, Lindl., var. Walteri.
3. gracilis, Bigelow.
4. simplex, Gray.   E. Greenwich, *Congdon.*

LISTERA, R. Br. Twayblade.
cordata, R. Br.   So. Kingstown.

ARETHUSA, Gronov.

bulbosa, L.

POGONIA, Juss.

1. **ophioglossoides,** Nutt.
2. **pendula,** Lindl.   Foster, Glocester.
3. **verticellata,** Nutt.   N. Providence, Providence, *Bailey.*

CALOPOGON, R. Br.

pulchellus, R. Br.

MICROSTYLIS, Nutt. ADDER'S MOUTH.
ophioglossoides, Nutt.   Exeter, *Prof. Bailey.*

LIPARIS, Richard. TWAYBLADE.

1. **liliifolia,** Richard.
2. **Loeselii,** Richard.   Extremely rare.

CORALLORHIZA, Haller. CORAL ROOT.

1. **odontorhiza,** Nutt.
2. **multiflora,** Nutt.

CYPRIPEDIUM, L. LADIES' SLIPPER.

1. **parviflorum,** Salisb.   *Olney.*
2. **pubescens,** Willd.   Johnston, &c.
3. **acaule,** Ait.

ORDER 92. **AMARYLLIDACEÆ.**

HYPOXYS, L. STAR GRASS.

erecta, L.

ORDER 93. **HÆMODORACEÆ.**

LACHNANTHES, L. RED ROOT.
tinctoria, Ell.   Worden's Pond, &c.

ALETRIS, L. COLIC ROOT.
farinosa, L.

ORDER 94. **IRIDACEÆ.**

IRIS, L. IRIS, FLEUR DE LYS.

1. **versicolor,** L.
2. **Virginica,** L.

SISYRINCHIUM, L. BLUE EYED GRASS.
auceps, Cav.

ORDER 95. **DIOSCOREACEÆ.**

DIOSCOREA, Plumier. YAM.

villosa, L. Washington County, Providence.

ORDER 96. **SMILACEÆ.**

SMILAX, Tourn. GREEN-BRIER.

1. rotundifolia, L.
   var. quadrangularis. Potawomut, &c.
2. glauca, Walt. East Greenwich, *Congdon;* Quidnessett, &c.
3. herbacea, L. CARRION FLOWER.

ORDER 97. **LILIACEÆ.**

TRILLIUM, L.

1. erectum, L. BIRTH-ROOT.
   var. album. YELLOW BIRTH-ROOT.
2. cernuum, L. WAKE ROBIN.
3. erythrocarpum, Michx. Cumberland, South Kingstown, *Leland.*

MEDEOLA, Gronov. CUCUMBER-ROOT.

Virginica, L.

MELANTHIUM, L.

Virginicum, L. *Olney.*

VERATRUM, Tourn. FALSE HELLEBORE.

viride, Ait.

UVULARIA, L. BELLWORT.

1. perfoliata, L.
2. sessilifolia, L.

CLINTONIA, Raf.

borealis, Raf.

SMILACINA, Desf. FALSE SOLOMON SEAL.

1. racemosa, Desf.
2. stellata, Desf.
3. trifolia, Desf. Johnston, *Congdon.*
4. bifolia, Ker., var. Canadensis.

POLYGONATUM, Tourn. SOLOMON'S SEAL.

1. biflorum, Ell.
2. giganteum, Dietrich. Gloucester, Burrillville.

ASPARAGUS, L.

officinalis, L.

LILIUM, L. Lily.

1. **Philadelphicum,** L.
2. **Canadense,** L.
3. **superbum,** L. Turk's Cap.

ERYTHRONIUM, L.
Americanum, Smith. Dog's Tooth Violet.

ORNITHOGALUM, Tourn.
umbellatum, L. Star of Bethlehem.

ALLIUM, L. Wild Onion.

1. **tricoccum,** Ait.
2. **Canadense,** Kalm.
3. **vineale,** L.   Cranston, *Bennett.*

HEMEROCALLIS, L. Day Lily.
fulva, L.

Order 98. JUNCACEÆ.

LUZULA, D. C. Wood-Rush.

1. **pilosa,** Willd.
2. **campestris,** D. C.

JUNCUS, L. Bay-Rush.

1. **effusus,** L.
2. **Balticus,** Dethard.   Stone Bridge, *Congdon.*
3. **marginatus,** Rostk.
4. **Gerardi,** Loisel.
5. **bufonius,** L.
6. **tenuis,** Willd.
7. **Greenei,** Oakes & Tuckerman.
8. **pelocarpus,** E. Meyer.
9. **articulatus,** L.
10. **militaris,** Bigelow.
    var. ———, with long capillary leaves. Wood River, *Bennett.*
11. **acuminatus,** Michx.
    var. **debilis.**
    var. **legitimus.**
12. **nodosus,** L.
13. **scirpoides,** Lam.
14. **Canadensis,** J. Gay. var. **longicaudatus.**
    var. **subcaudatus.** Quidnessett, *Bennett.*

Order 99. PONTEDERIACEÆ.

PONTEDERIA, L. Pickerel-Weed.
cordata, L. Blue Arrow-Head.

Order 100. **XYRIDACEÆ.**
XYRIS, L. Yellow-Eyed Grass.
1. flexuosa, Willd.
2. Caroliniana, Walt.

Order 101. **ERIOCAULONACEÆ.**
ERIOCAULON, L. Pipewort.
septangulare, With.

Order 102. **CYPERACEÆ.**
CYPERUS, L. Galingale.
1. flavescens, L.
2. diandrus, Torr.
3. Nuttallii, Torr.
4. inflexus, Muhl.
5. dentatus, Torr.
6. phymatodes, Muhl.
7. strigosus, L.
8. Michauxianus, Schultze. Block Island, *Olney ;* Quidnessett. *Bennett.*
9. Grayii, Torr.
10. filiculmis, Vahl.

DULICHIUM, Richard.
spathaceum, Pers.

FUIRENA, Rottboell. Umbrella Grass.
squarrosa, Michx.   Benedict Pond.
    var. **pumila.**   Worden's Pond, *Bennett.*

HEMICARPHA, Nees.
subsquarrosa, Nees.   Long Pond, Providence.

ELEOCHARIS, R. Br. Spike-Rush.
1. Robbinsii, Oakes.
2. equisetoides, Torr.   Cumberland, *Olney ;* Cranston.
3. tuberculosa, R. Br.
4. obtusa, Schultze.
5. olivacea, Torr.   Providence, E. Greenwich.
6. palustris, R. Br.
7. rostellata, Torr.   Quidnessett, Field's Point.
8. tenuis, Schultze.
9. melanocarpa, Torr.
10. acicularis, R. Br.
11. pygmæa, Torr.   Seekonk River, &c.

SCIRPUS, L.
1. planifolius, Muhl.

2. subterminalis, Torr.
3. pungens, Vahl.
4. Olneyi, Gray.   Providence.
5. Torreyi, Olney.
6. validus, Vahl.
7. debilis, Pursh.
8. Smithii, Gray.   S. Kingstown, *Congdon.*
9. maritimus, L.
            var. macrostachys.
10. fluviatilis, Gray.
11. sylvaticus, L.
12. atrovirens, Muhl.
13. polyphyllus, Vahl.
14. Eriophorum, Michx.

ERIOPHORUM, L. COTTON GRASS.

1. Virginicum, L.
2. polystachyon, L.
3. gracile, Koch.

FIMBRISTYLIS, Vahl.

1. autumnalis, R. & S.
2. capillaris, Gray.

RHYNCHOSPORA, Vahl. BEAK-RUSH.

1. scirpoides, Gray.
2. fusca, R. & S.
3. alba, Vahl.
4. glomerata, Vahl.
5. macrostachya, Torr.

CLADIUM, P. Browne. TWIG-RUSH.

mariscoides, Torr.

SCLERIA, L. NUT-RUSH.

1. triglomerata, Michx.   Warwick, *Congdon.*
2. reticularis, Michx.
3. laxa, Torr.

CAREX, L. SEDGE.

1. polytrichoides, Muhl.
2. bromoides, Schk.
3. siccata, Dew.
4. teretiuscula, Good.
5. vulpinoidea, Michx.
6. stipata, Muhl.
7. muricata, L.   Stone Bridge, *Congdon.*
8. sparganiodes, Muhl.

9. **cephaloidea,** Dew.   Warwick, *Congdon.*
10. **cephalophora,** Muhl
11. **Muhlenbergii,** Schk.
12. **rosea,** Schk.
13. **retroflexa,** Muhl.   Cumberland, *Olney.*
14. **trisperma,** Dew.
15. **canescens,** L.
16. **Deweyana,** Schw.   *J. W. Congdon, Esq.*
17. **exilis,** Dew.
18. **sterilis,** Willd.
19. **stellulata,** L.
        var. **scirpoides.**
20. **scoparia,** Schk.
        var. **minor,** Boott.
21. **lagopodiodes,** Schk.
22. **cristata,** Schw.
        var. **mirabilis,** Boott.
23. **adusta,** Boott.
24. **fœnea,** Willd.
25. **silicea,** Olney.
        C. fœnea, var? sabulonum.
26. **straminea,** Schk., var. **typica.**
            var. **tenera,** Boott.
            var. **aperta,** Boott.
            var. **festucacea,** Boott.
            var. **minor.**
27. **alata,** Torr.   *Mr. William Boott.*
28. **vulgaris,** Fries.   Middletown, &c.
29. **torta.** Boott.
30. **aperta,** Boott.
        var. ——, Boott.   *Olney.*
31. **Virginiana,** Sm.
        C. stricta, Lam.
32. **strictior,** Dew.
        C. stricta, var. strictior.
33. **crinita,** Lam.
34. **gynandra,** Schw.
35. **Mitchelliana,** M. A. Curtis.
36. **limosa,** L.   Johnston, Quidnessett. *Bennett.*
37. **Buxbaumii,** Wahl.
38. **aurea,** Nutt.   *J. W. Congdon, Esq.*
39. **panicea,** L. & vars.
40. **pallescens,** L.
41. **conoidea,** Schk.
42. **grisea,** Wahl.   Quidnessett, *Bennett.*
43. **gracillima,** Schw.
44. **virescens,** Muhl.
45. **triceps,** Michx.
    4

46. **platyphylla,** Carey.   Cumberland, Rocky Point, *Bennett.*
47. **retrocurva,** Dew.
48. **digitalis,** Willd.
49. **laxiflora,** Lam.
     var. **plantaginea.**
     var. **intermedia.**
50. **blanda,** Dew.
     C. laxiflora, var. blanda.
     var. **major.**
     var. **minor.**
51. **umbellata,** Schk.
52. **Novæ-Angliæ,** Schw.
53. **Emmonsii,** Dew.
     var. **elliptica,** Boott.
54. **Pennsylvanica,** Lam.
55. **varia,** Muhl.
56. **pubescens,** Muhl.
57. **miliacea,** Muhl.
58. **scabrata,** Schw.
59. **debilis,** Michx.
60. **flava,** L.
61. **filiformis,** L.
62. **lanuginosa,** Michx.   Field's Point, *Congdon.*
63. **vestita,** Willd.
64. **polymorpha,** Muhl.   N. Providence, *Olney.*
65. **striata,** Michx.
66. **riparia,** Curtis.   E. Providence, *Congdon.*
67. **Pseudo-Cyperus,** L.
     var. **comosa,** Boott.
     C. comosa, Boott.
68. **hystricina,** Willd.
69. **tentaculata,** Muhl.
     var. **altior.**
70. **intumescens,** Rudge.
71. **lupulina,** Muhl.
72. **lupuliformis,** Sartwell.   Quidnessett, *Bennett.*
73. **subulata,** Michx.   Worden's Pond, *Olney.*
74. **utriculata,** Boott.
     var. **minor,** Boott.
75. **Olneyi,** Boott.   Cat-Swamp. *Strictly local.*
76. **Tuckermani,** Boott.
77. **bullata,** Schk.
78. **monile,** Tuckerm.
     var. **minor,** Olney

ORDER 103. **GRAMINEÆ.**

PASPALUM, L.

1. setacum, Michx.
2. laeve, Mx.

PANICUM, L. PANIC GRASS.

1. filiforme, L.
2. glabrum, Gaud.
3. sanguinale, L.
4. virgatum, L.
5. amarum, Ell.
6. agrostoides, Spreng.
7. proliferum, Lam.
8. capillare, L.
9. miliaceum, L.
10. latifolium, L.
11. clandestinum, L. & vars.
12. microcarpum, Muhl. Warwick, *Congdon ;* Johnston, *Bennett.*
13. pauciflorum, Ell.
14. dichotomum, L.
15. laxiflorum, Lam.
    C. dichotomum, var.
16. ramulosum, Mx.
    C. dichotomum, var.
17. depauperatum, Muhl.
18. verrucosum, Muhl.   Field's Point, E. Providence, &c.
19. Crus-Galli, L. COCK'S-COMB GRASS.
           var. hispidum.

SETARIA, Beauv. BRISTLY FOX-TAIL GRASS.

1. verticillata, Beauv.
2. glauca, Beauv.
3. viridis, Beauv.
4. Italica, Kth.

CENCHRUS, L. BURR GRASS.

tribuloides. L.

SPARTINA, Schreber. CORD GRASS.

1. cynosuroides, Willd.
2. polystachyon, Willd.
3. juncea, Willd.
4. stricta, Roth, & vars.

TRIPSACUM, L. GAMA GRASS, SESAME.

dactyloides, L.   E. Providence, Rocky Point, &c.
           var. monostachyum.   Field's Point.

ZIZANIA, Gronov. WILD RICE.
aquatica, L.

LEERSIA, Solander. WHITE GRASS.
1. **Virginica**, Willd.
2. **oryzoides**, Swartz.

ANDROPOGON, L. BEARD-GRASS.
1. **provincialis**, Lam.
   A. furcatus, Muhl.
2. **scoparius**, Michx.
3. **dissitiflorus**, Mx.   Washington County.
   A. Virginicus, L.

CHRYSOPOGON, Trin. BROOM-CORN.
nutans, Benth.
   Sorghum nutans, Gray.

PHALARIS, L. CANARY-GRASS.
1. **Canariensis**, L.
2. **arundinacea**, L.

ANTHOXANTHUM, L.
odoratum, L. JUNE GRASS.

HIEROCHLOE, Gmelin. HOLY-GRASS.
borealis, R. & S. VANILLA-GRASS.

ALOPECURUS, L. FOX-TAIL.
1. **pratensis**, L.
2. **geniculatus**, L.
   var. **aristulatus.**
   A. aristulatus, Michx.

ARISTIDA, L.
1. **dichotoma**, Mx. POVERTY GRASS.
2. **gracilis**, Ell.   E. Greenwich, *Congdon;* Providence, *Bennett.*
3. **purpurascens**, Poir.   N. Kingstown, &c.

STIPA, L. FEATHER GRASS.
avenacea, L.

ORYZOPSIS, Michx. MOUNTAIN RICE.
1. **melanocarpa**, Muhl.   Smithfield, &c.
2. **asperifolia**, Mx.   N. Providence, Johnston.
3. **Canadensis**, Torr.

MILIUM, L. Millet Grass.

effusum, L.   *S. T. Olney.*

MUHLENBERGIA, Schreber. Drop Seed Grass.

1. sobolifera, Trin.
2. glomerata, Trin.
3. Mexicana, Trin. & vars.
4. sylvatica, T. & G.
5. Willdenovii, Trin.   *J. W. Congdon, Esq.*
9. diffusa, Schreb.
7. capillaris, Kth.   Providence streets, *Bennett.*

BRACHELYTRUM, Beauv.

aristatum, Beauv.

PHLEUM, L. Cat's-Tail Grass.

pratense, L. Timothy.

SPOROBOLUS, R. Br.

1. asper, Kth. Rush Grass.
                 Vilfa aspera, Beauv.
2. vaginæflora, Torr.
                 Vilfa vaginæflora, Torr.
3. serotina, Gray. Dropseed Grass.

AGROSTIS, L. Bent.

1. perennans, Tuckerm. Thin Grass.
2. scabra, Willd. Hair Grass.
3. canina, L. R. I. Bent.
4. vulgaris, With. Red-Top, Herds Grass.
                 var. alba. White Bent.
                 A. alba, L.

CINNA, L. Wood Reed-Grass.

arundinacea, L. & vars.

DEYEUXIA, Kunth. Reed Bent Grass.

1. Canadensis, Beauv.
                 Calamagrostis, —.
2. Nuttalliana, Steud.
                 Calamagrostis, —.

AMMOPHILA, Host. Sea-Sand Reed.

arenaria, Roth.
                 Calamagrostis, —.

DESCHAMPSIA, Beauv. Hair Grass.

flexuosa, L.
                 Aira, —.

HOLCUS, L. Meadow Soft Grass.
lanatus, L.

TRISETUM, Pers.
palustre, L.

ARRHENATHERUM, Beauv. Oat Grass.
avenaceum, Beauv.

DANTHONIA, D. C. Wild Oat Grass.
1. spicata, Beauv.
2. sericea, Nutt.

ELEUSINE, Gaertn. Crab-Grass.
Indica, Gaertn.   Providence, *Bennett.*

DIPLACHNE, Beauv.
fascicularis, Beauv.
> *Leptochloa fascicularis, Gray.*

TRIPLASIS, Beauv.
purpurea, Chapm.
> *Tricuspis purpurea, Gray.*

PHRAGMITIS, Trin. Reed.
communis, Trin.

EATONIA, Raf.
1. obtusata, Gray.   Manville. *Congdon.*
2. Pennsylvanica, Gray.

ERAGROSTIS, Beauv.
1. minor, Host.   S. Providence, &c.
> *E. poœoides, Beauv.*
2. major, Host.
> *E. poœoides, var. megastachya.*
3. pilosa, Beauv.
4. capillaris, Nees.
5. pectinacea, Gray.
> var. spectabilis.

DISTICHLIS, Raf. Spike-Grass.
maritima, Raf.
> *Brizopyrum spicatum, Hook.*

DACTYLIS, L. Orchard-Grass.
glomerata, L.

POA, L. Meadow-Grass, Spear-Grass.

1. annua, L.
2. compressa, L.
3. serotina, Ehrh. Fowl Meadow-Grass.
4. pratensis, L. Kentucky Blue Grass.
5. trivialis, L.
6. debilis, Torr.

GLYCERIA, R. Br. Manna Grass.

1. Canadensis, Trin. Rattlesnake Grass.
2. obtusa, Trin.
3. nervata, Trin.
4. pallida, Trin. Rocky Point.
5. aquatica, Sm., var. Americana, Vasey. Reed Meadow Grass.
6. fluitans, R. Br.
7. acutiflora, Torr.
8. maritima, Wahl. Sea Spear-Grass.
9. distans, Wahl.

BRIZA, L. Quaking Grass.

media, L. Waste places.

FESTUCA, L. Fescue.

1. tenella, Willd.
2. Myurus, L. E. Providence, &c.
3. ovina, L. Sheep's Fescue.
4. duriuscula, L.
   F. ovina, var.
5. rubra, L.
   F. ovina, var.
6. nutans, Willd.

BROMUS, L. Brome Grass.

1. secalinus, L. Cheat or Chess.
2. racemosus, L.
3. mollis, L.
4. ciliatus, L.
   var. purgans.
5. sterilis, L.
6. tectarum, L.

LOLIUM, L. Darnel.

perenne, L.

AGROPYRUM, Beauv. Wheat.

1. repens, Beauv.
   Triticum, ——, L.
   var? ——. Allen's Harbor, Nayatt.

2. **caninum**, R. & S.
          Triticum, —, L.
     ELYMUS, L. WILD RYE.
1. **Virginicus**, L.
2. **Canadensis**, L.
3. **striatus**, Willd.
          var. **villosus**.   Rocky Point, &c.
     ASPRELLA,   BOTTLE-BRUSH GRASS.
hystrix, Willd.
          Gymnostichum Hystrix, Schreb.

SERIES II.

CRYPTOGAMIA.

CLASS III. ACROGENS.

ORDER 104. EQUISETACEÆ.

     EQUISETUM, L. HORSE-TAIL, SCOURING RUSH.
1. **arvense**, L.
2. **sylvaticum**, L.
3. **limosum**, L.
4. **hyemale**, L.

ORDER 105. FILICES.

     POLYPODIUM, L. POLYPOD.
vulgare, L.
          var. **Cambricum.?**   Westerly.
     PTERIS, L. BRAKE, BRACKEN.
aquilina, L.

     ADIANTUM, L. MAIDEN-HAIR.
pedatum, L.*

     WOODWARDIA, Smith. CHAIN FERN.
1. **Virginica**, Smith.
2. **angustifolia**, Smith.

     CAMPTOSURUS, Link. WALKING FERN.
rhizophyllus, Link.   One locality only known.

          * *A. cuneatum, Kaulf.* Maintained itself and grew profusely for several
seasons in Cumberland, but at last died out.

ASPLENIUM, L. Spleenwort.

1. Trichomanes, L.
2. Ebeneum, Ait.
3. thelypteroides, Michx.
4. Filix-fœmina, Bernh.

PHEGOPTERIS, Fee. Beech Fern.

1. polypodioides, Fee.
2. hexagonoptera, Fee.
3. Dryopteris, Fee & var.

ASPIDIUM, Swartz. Shield Fern.

1. Thelypteris, Swartz.
2. Noveboracense, Swartz.
3. spinulosum, Swartz, var. intermedium.
                          var. Boottii.
4. cristatum, Swartz.
            var. Clintonianum.   Cranston, *Bennett.*
5. marginale, Swartz.
6. acrostichoides, Swartz.
            var. incisum.

CYSTOPTERIS, Bernhardi. Bladder Fern.

1. bulbifera, Bernh.
2. fragilis, Bernh.
            var. dentata, Hook.   E. Greenwich, *Bennett.*

ONOCLEA, L.

1. Germanica, Hook. Ostrich Fern. *First detected by Mr. Hunt.*
            Struthiopteris, —, *Willd.*
2. sensibilis, L. Sensitive Fern.
            var. obtusilobata.   Hill's Grove, *Bennett.*

WOODSIA, R. Br.

1. obtusa, Torr.
2. Ilvensis, R. Br.

DICKSONIA, L'Her.

punctilobula, Kze.

LYGODIUM, Swartz. Climbing Fern.

palmatum, Swartz.

OSMUNDA, L. Flowering Fern.

1. regalis, L. Pride of the Meadows.
2. Claytoniana, L.
3. cinnamomea, L.
            var. frondosa.   Johnston.

BOTRYCHIUM, Swartz. Moonwort.

1. **Virginicum,** Swartz.
2. **ternatum,** Swartz, var. **lunarioides,** Milde.
   B. lunarioides.
   var. **obliquum,** Milde.
   B. lunarioides, var.
   var. **dissectum,** Milde.
   B. lunarioides, var.

OPHIOGLOSSUM, L. Adder's Tongue.

vulgare, L.   Rare and local.

ORDER 106. **LYCOPODIACEÆ.**

LYCOPODIUM, L. Club Moss.

1. **lucidulum,** Michx.
2. **inundatum,** L., var.   Washington County.
3. **annotinum,** L.   *Olney.*
4. **dendroideum,** Michx. Ground-Pine.
5. **clavatum,** L. Lion's Paw.
6. **complanatum,** L. Creeping Jenny.

SELAGINELLA, Beauv.

1. **rupestris,** Spring.
2. **apus,** Spring.

ISOETES, L. Quillwort.

1. **lacustris,** L.
2. **Tuckermani,** Braun.   E. Greenwich, *Congdon.*
3. **echinospora,** Durieu.   Davisville, *Bennett.*
4. **riparia,** Engelm.   Apponaug. *Congdon.*
5. **Engelmanni,** Braun.   Davisville; Newport, *Dr. Farlow.*

ORDER 107. **CHARACEÆ.**

CHARA, (L.) Ag.

1. **coronata,** var. **Schweinitzii.**   Newport, *Dr. Farlow.*
2. **vulgaris,** L.
3. **fragilis,** Desv.
4. **Hydropitys,** A. Br., var. **septentrionavis.** Gorton's Pond.
5. **sejuncta,** A. Br.   Apponaug, *Mr. E. Faxon.*

NITELLA, Ag.

1. **gracilis,** Ag.
2. **intermedia,** Adst.   Apponaug. *Dr. Allen.*
3. **tenuissima,** Desv. (Kutz.)   *Dr. Allen.*

CLASS IV. ANOPHYTÆ.

ORDER 108. MUSCI.

SPHAGNUM, Dill.

1. acutifolium, Ehrh.   Swamps and bogs.
    var. purpureum, Schimp.   "   "
    var. fuscum, Schimp.   "   "
2. cuspidatum, Ehrh.   "   "
    var. falcatum, Russ.   "   "
    var. plumosum, Schimp.   "   "
3. intermedium. Hoffm.   Shady bogs.
4. squarrosum, Pers.   "   "
5. rigidum, Schimp.   *C. F. Austin.*
6. subsecundum, Nees, var. contortum, Schimp. Swamps and bogs.
7. cymbifolium, Ehrh.   Swamps and bogs.
8. papillosum, Lindb.   "   "
9. macrophyllum, Bernh.?   Stagnant marsh, Quidnessett.

EPHEMERUM, Hampe.

1. serratum, Hampe.   On the ground in fields.
2. crassinervium, Hampe.   Moist ground.
3. spinulosum, Br. & Sch.   "   "
4. cohærens, Muhl.   "   "

SPHÆRANGIUM, Schimp.

1. rufescens, Schimp.   On moist ground.
2. triquetrum, Schimp.   On the ground in fields.

PHASCUM, L.

cuspidatum, Schreb.   On the ground in fields.

PLEURIDIUM, Brid.

1. Ravenelli, Austin.   Fields Quidnessett, *Bennett.*
2. alternifolium, Brid.   Fields.

BRUCHIA, Schwaegr.

1. flexuosa, Muell.   Clayey ground.
2. Sullivantii, Aust.   "   "
3. brevipes, Hook.?   Providence, damp ground.

WEISIA, Hedw.

viridula, Brid.   On damp ground.
 var. gymnostomoides, Muell.   "   "

CYNODONTIUM, Br. & Sch.

gracilescens, Schimp.   In rocky woods.

DICRANELLA, Schimp.

1. cerviculata, Schimp.   In damp places.
2. varia, Schimp.   In wet woods.
3. rufescens, Schimp.   In heavy soil.
4. subulata, Schimp.   In shady wood.
5. heteromalla, Schimp.   On clayey land.

DICRANUM, Hedw.

1. Starkii, Web & Mohr.   In rocky woods.
2. flagellare, Hedw.   On rotten logs in the shade.
3. fulvum, Hook.   In rocky woods.
4. longifolium, Hedw.   On trees.
5. fuscescens, Turner.   In woods on trees.
6. scoparium, Hedw. & vars. On trees and rocks and the ground.
7. Schraderi, W. & M.   Shady wet places.
8. spurium, Hedw.   On poor soil.
9. undulatum, Turn.   Wet shady places.

FISSIDENS, Hedw.

1. exiguus, Sull.   On wet rocky places.
2. minutulus, Sull.   "   "   "
3. taxifolius, Hedw.   Wet shady spots.
4. adiantoides, Hedw.   Wet open ground.

CONOMITRIUM, Mont.

Julianum, Mont.   Damp woods.

LEUCOBRYUM, Hampe.

vulgare, Hampe.   In woods.

CERATODON, Brid.

purpureus, Brid.   On open ground.
    var. aristatus. Austin.

POTTIA, Ehrb.

truncata, Fuern.   In old fields.

LEPTOTRICHUM, Hampe.

1. tortile, Muell.   Sandy land.
2. vaginans, Sull.   Damp clayey banks.
3. pallidum, Hampe.   Shady woods.

BARBULA, Hedw.

1. unguiculata, Hedw.   In heavy land.
2. cæspitosa, Schwaegr.   In shady woods on trees.

3. **tortuosa**, Web. & Mohr.   *Austin.*
4. **papillosa**, Muell.   Providence on Elm trees.

GRIMMIA, Ehrh.

1. **(Schistidium) apocarpa**, Heau.   Upon rocks.
            var. **gracilis**, N. & H.   "
            var. **rivularis**, N. & H.   On wet rocks.
2. **Olneyi**, Sull.   On granite rocks.

RACOMITRIUM, Br. & Sch.

canescens, Brid.   Warwick, *Bennett.*   On rocks.

HEDWIGIA, Ehrh.

ciliata, Ehrh. & vars.   On rocks.

DRUMMONDIA, Hook.

clavellata, Hook.   Upon trees.

ULOTA, Mohr.

1. **crispa**, Brid.   Upon rocks.
2. **crispula**, Brid.   *Austin.*
3. **Hutchinsiæ**, Schimp.   On rocks and trees.

ORTHOTRICHUM, Hedw.

1. **sordidum**, Sull. & Lesqx.   On trees in wet woods.
2. **Ohioense**, Sull. & Lesqx.   On trees.
3. **strangulatum**, Beauv.   On trees and rocks.
4. **obtusifolium**, Schrad.   On trees, *fide Austin.*

TETRAPHIS, Hedw.

pellucida, Hedw.   On decayed logs in shade.

APHANORHEGMA, Sulliv.

serratum, Sull.   In clayey shady spots.

PHYSCOMITRIUM, Brid.

pyriforme, Brid.   In old fields by wall sides, &c.

FUNARIA, Schreb.

hygrometricum, Schth.   On ground.
     var. **calvescens**. Br. & Sch.   In a few places.

BARTRAMIA, Hedw.

pomiformis, Hedw.   On shady hill-sides.

PHILONOTIS, Brid.

1. **Muhlenbergii**, Brid.   In springy places.
2. **fontana**, Brid.   In same positions as last.

LEPTOBRYUM, Schimp.

pyriforme, Schimp.   In light soil in shady places.

WEBERA, Hedw.

1. **nutans,** Hedw.   Moist shady soil.
2. **annotina,** Schwaegr.   Rocky woods.
3. **albicans,** Schimp.   Swampy places.

BRYUM, Br. & Sch.

1. **pendulum,** Schimp.   On rocks and logs in woods.
2. **intermedium,** Brid.   On rocks.
3. **bimum,** Schreb.   In wet woods.
4. **argenteum,** L.   In open places.
         var. **majus,** Schwaegr.   In shady spots.
         var. **lanatum,** Br. & Sch. In dry sunny places.
5. **cæspiticium,** L.   In open land.
6. **capillare,** L.   In shady wet woods.
7. **pseudo-triquetrum,** Schwaegr.   In springy places.
8. **roseum,** Schreb.   In dry woods on trees and rocks.

MNIUM, Br. & Sch.

1. **cuspidatum,** Hedw.   In woods at roots of trees.
2. **affine,** Bland.   In same places.
3. **hornum,** L.   Brook side " Grotto," Providence.
4. **stellare,** Reich.   Shady banks.
5. **cinclidoides,** Hueber.   Swamps.
6. **punctatum,** Hedw.   Swamps.

AULACOMNION, Schwaegr.

1. **palustre,** Schwaegr & vars.   In swamps.
2. **heterostichum,** Br. & Sch.   In wet places.

POGONATUM, Beauv.

brevicaule, Beauv.   On ground.

POLYTRICHUM, Brid.

1. **formosum,** Hedw.   In woods at foot of trees.
2. **piliferum,** Schreb.   In open places.
3. **Juniperinum,** Willd.   In poor soil.
4. **commune,** L.   In woods and also open places.
         var. **perigoniale,** Br. & Sch.   In same places.

ATRICHUM, Beauv.

1. **angustatum,** Beauv.   In shady woods.
2. **undulatum,** Beauv.   On ground or dry stumps.

DIPHYSCIUM, Web. & Mohr.

foliosum, Mohr.   Damp clayey ground.

BUXBAUMIA, Haller.

aphylla, L.   On ground, Pleasant Valley.

FONTINALIS, Dill.

1. **antipyretica**, L.   In brooks.
   var. **gigantea**, Sulliv.   Pleasant Valley brook, &c.
2. **Dalecarlica**, Br. & Sch.   In running water.
3. **biformis**, Sulliv.   In streams in woods.
4. **Novæ-Angliæ**, Sulliv.   In brooks.
5. **Lescurii**, var. **gracilescens**, Sulliv.   In brooks.

DICHELYMA, Myrin.

1. **falcatum**, Myrin.   In swamps and brooks.
2. **capillaceum**, Br. & Sch.   In swamps.

NECKERA, Hedw.

1. **pennata**, Hedw.   On trees.
2. **complanata**, Hueber.   On rocks.

HOMALIA, Brid.

? **trichomanoides**, Br. & Sch. ?   *Coe F. Austin.*

LEUCODON, Schwaegr.

1. **julaceus**, Sulliv.   On trees.
2. **brachypus**, Brid.   On trees.

PTERIGYNANDRUM, Hedw.

filiforme, Hedw.   On trees and rocks.

THELIA, Sullivant.

1. **hirtella**, Sulliv.   On trees.
2. **asprella**, Sulliv.   On trees.
3. **Lescurii**, Sulliv.   On trees and ground.

LESKEA, Hedw.

1. **polycarpa**, Ehrh.   On trees.
2. **obscura**, Hedw.   On trees in swamps.
3. **tristis**, Cesat.   On trees in swamps.

ANOMODON, Hook & Tayl.

1. **rostratus**, Schimp.   On trees.
2. **attenuatus**, Hueben.   On trees and ground.
3. **obtusifolius**, Br. & Sch.   On trees in swamps.

PLATYGYRIUM, Bry. Eur.

repens, Br. & Sch.　　　　　　On rotten wood in shade.

PYLAISÆA, Bry. Eur.

1. subdenticulata, var. obscura, Schimp.　On the ground in woods.
2. intricata, Br. & Sch.　　　In woods on trees and stumps.
3. velutina, Br. & Sch.　　　　　　　　　　On trees.

HOMALOTHECIUM, Bry. Eur.

subcapillatum, Sulliv.　　　　　On trunks of trees.

CYLINDROTHECIUM, Bry. Eur.

1. cladorhizans, Schimp.　　　On rotten logs in swamp.
2. seductrix, Sulliv.　　　　　　　In same places.

CLIMACIUM, Web. & Mohr.

Americanum, Brid.　　　　　　　In swamps.

HYPNUM, Dill.

1. (Thuidium) minutulum, Hedw.　On tree bases in woods.
2. 　　　　scitum, Beauv., var. æstivale.　　On same.
3. 　　　　tamariscinum, Hedw. ?　　In wet places.
4. 　　　　recognitum, Hedw.　　In same situation.
5. 　　　　delicatulum, L.　On trees in same situation.
6. 　　　　abietinum, L.　　On ground in shade.
7. (Elodium) paludosum, Sull.　　In marshy places.
8. (Camptothecium) nitens, Schreb.　In swamps and bogs.
9. (Brachythecium) lætum, Brid.　On ground and wet logs.
10. 　　　　acuminatum, Beauv.　　In same situation.
11. 　　　　salebrosum, Hoffm. & vars.　In same situation.
12. 　　　　velutinum, L.　On ground in damp shades.
13. 　　　　rutabulum, L. & vars.　In similar situations.
14. 　　　　plumosum, Swartz.　On stones in damp woods.
15. (Eurhynchium) strigosum, Hoffm.　　In woods.
16. 　　　　diversifolium, Schimp.　On shady banks.
17. 　　　　Boscii, Schwaegr.　On the ground in woods.
18. 　　　　hians, Hedw.　　In shady woods.
19. 　　　　Sullivantii, Spruce.　In wet shady places.
20. (Rhapidostegium) demissum, Wils.　Damp rocks.
21. 　　　　recurvans, Schwaegr.　Wet bogs in woods.
22. (Rhynchostegium) deplanatum, Schimp.　On ground in woods.
23. 　　　　serrulatum, Hedw.　On ground in woods, &c.
24. 　　　　rusciforme, Weis. & vars.　In brooks on stones.
25. (Plagiothecium) turfaceum, Lindberg.　On rotten logs in swamps.
26. 　　　　denticulatum, L., & vars.　On rotten logs.
27. 　　　　Muhlenbeckii, Spruce.　On ground and rocks.
28. (Amblystegium) subtile, Hoffm.　At foot of trees.
29. 　　　　serpens, L.　　In damp spots on logs.

30.	**(Amblystegium) radicale,** Beauv.	In shady wet places.
31.	**orthocladon,** Beauv.	In wet places.
32.	**adnatum,** Hedw.	On trees and rocks in shade.
33.	**riparium,** L. & vars.	In swamps
34.	**(Campylium) hispidulum,** Brid.	On trees in swamps.
35.	**chrysophyllum,** Brid.	*Fide Austin.*
36.	**stellatum,** Schreb.	On rotten wood in swamps.
37.	**polygamum,** Wils.	In swamps.
38.	**(Harpidium) aduncum,** Hedw. & vars.	Bogs and swamps.
39.	**uncinatum,** Hedw. & vars.	Bogs and swamps.
40.	**fluitans,** L. & vars.	In stagnant places.
41.	**exannulatum,** Guembel.	In swamp, Quidnessett.
42.	**(Ctenium) Crista-Castrensis,** L.	In woods.
43.	**(Ctenidium) molluscum,** Hedw.	In woods.
44.	**(Hypnum) reptile,** var. **protuberans,** Michx.	On trees.
45.	**imponens,** Hedw.	On roots of trees.
46.	**cupressiforme,** L. & vars.	On trees and rocks.
47.	**curvifolium,** Hedw.	On decayed logs in woods.
48.	**Haldanianum,** Grev.	On logs in wet places.
49.	**(Calliergon) cordifolium,** Hedw.	In swamps and bogs.
50.	**cuspidatum,** L.	In stagnant swamps.
51.	**Schreberi,** Willd.	In woods on ground.
52.	**stramineum,** Dicks.	In swamps and bogs.
53.	**(Pleurozium) splendens,** Hedw.	On ground in woods.
54.	**brevirostre,** Ehrh.	*Fide Austin.*
55.	**(Hylocomium) triquetrum,** L.	On ground in shady spots.

5

ORDER 109. HEPATICÆ, (Musci hepatici.)

RICCIA, Mich.

1. lamellosa, Raddi. — Damp wood paths in light soil.
2. arvensis, Austin. — Shady sterile earth.
3. lutescens, Schwein. — In ditches infertile.
4. fluitans, L. & vars. — In standing water and by ditch sides.
5. natans, L. — Stagnant places.

MARCHANTIA, Raddi.
polymorpha, L. — Shady damp spots.

PREISSIA, Corda.
hemisphærica, Cogn. — In moist places.
    P. commutata, Nees.

GRIMALDIA, Raddi.
barbifrons, Bisch. — On the ground in fields.

ASTERELLA, Beauv.
hemisphærica, (Raddi.) — By brook sides.
    Reboulia, —, Raddi.

CONOCEPHALUS, Neck.
conicus, (Corda.) — Damp shady spots.
    Fegatella, —, Corda.

FIMBRIARIA, Nees.
tenella, Nees. — In damp shades.

LUNULARIA, Mich.
cruciata, Dmtr. — In hot beds around greenhouses.
    L. vulgaris, Mich.

ANTHOCEROS, L.

1. lævis, L. — In wet places.
2. punctatus, L. — In wet places.

NOTOTHYLAS, Sull.

1. orbicularis, Sull. — In damp spots.
2. melanospora, Sull. — In moist ground.

ANEURA, Dmtr.

1. multifida, Dmtr. — In wet places.
2. palmata, Nees. — On rotten stumps.
3. sessilis, Spreng. ? — C. F. Austin.
4. pinguis, Dmtr. — Among mosses and Peltigeras.
5. pinnatifida, Nees. — C. F. Austin.

PELLIA, Raddi.
epiphylla, (Corda.) Nees.   In damp ground.

BLASIA, Mich.
pusilla, L.   Ditches.

STEETZIA, Lehm.
Lyellii, Lehm.   Swamps.

METZGERIA, Raddi.
myriopoda, Lindb.   On rocks and trees.
> *M. furcata, Nees.*

FOSSOMBRONIA, Raddi.
1. pusilla, Nees.   Damp spots.
2. angulosa, Raddi.   Wet places.

FRULLANIA, Raddi.
1. Eboracensis,* Gottsche.   On rocks and trees.
2. squarrosa, Nees.   On trees.
3. plana, Sull.   On rocks.
4. Virginica, Gottsche.   Generally on trees.
5. Hutchinsiæ, Nees. var.   On stones.
6. Tamarisci, Nees.   On trees.
7. Grayana, Mont.   On trees and rocks.

LEJEUNIA, Lib.
1. serpyllifolia, Lib. var. Americana.   On wet rocks.
2. echinata, Taylor. Ms.   Found but once.
> *L. calcarea, Lib.*

PHRAGMICOMA, Dmtr.
clypeata, (Schwein.) Sull.   On rocks.
> *Lejeunia, —, Schwein.*

MADOTHECA, Dmtr.
1. Thuja, (Dicks.)   On rocks and trees.
2. platyphylla, Dmtr.   On trees.
3. Porella, Nees.   On rocks by brooksides.

RADULA, Nees.
1. complanata, Dmtr.   On roots of trees.
2. tenax, Lindb.   On rotten stumps.
> *R. pallens, Swtz.*

BLEPHAROZIA, Dmtr.
cilaris, Dmtr.   On rotten stumps.
> *Ptilidium, Nees.*

TRICHOCOLEA, Dmtr.
tomentella, Dmtr.   On earth and rotten logs.

---

* This includes F. saxatilis, Lindbg. of Sullivant in Gray's Manual.

BAZZANIA, B. Gr.

trilobata, (Nees.) B. Gr.   In shady places.
     Mastigobryum, —, *Nees.*

LEPIDOZIA, Nees.

1. **reptans,** Dmtr.   On the earth, seldom on rocks.
2. **setacea,** Mitt.   On the ground.
     Jungermannia, —, *Web.*

CALYPOGEIA, Raddi.

Trichomanes, Corda.   In wet and swampy places.

GEOCALYX, Nees.

graveolens, Nees.   Among Hypna in damp places.

CHILOSCYPHUS, Corda.

1. **ascendens,** Hook. & Wils.   On old stumps in swamps.
2. **polyanthos,** Corda.   On stones.
     var. **rivularis,** Nees.   On stones in wet places.

LOPHOCOLEA, Nees.

1. **bidentata,** Dmtr.   Swamps.
2. **minor,** Nees.   Roots and stumps.
3. **heterophylla,** Nees.   On rotting logs.
4. **crocata,** Nees.   Rare, found once in Lincoln, on log.

LIOCHLÆNA, Nees.

lanceolata, Nees.   C. F. Austin.

ODONTOSCHISMA, Dmtr.

denudata, Dmtr.   In swampy places.
     O. Huebneriana, Rab.

HARPANTHUS, Nees.

scutatus, Spruce.   On old wood.
     Jungermannia, —, *Web.*

CEPHALOZIA, Dmtr.

1. **multiflora,** Lindb.   On rotten logs.
     Jungermannia connivens, Dicks.
2. **divaricata,** Dmtr.   Light soil in shades.
3. **catenulata,** Lindbg.   On damp logs.
4. **curvifolia,** Dmtr.   On stumps, &c.
     Jungermannia, —, *Dicks.*

COLEOCHILA, Dmtr.

Taylori, (Hook.) Dmtr.   In bogs.
     Jungermannia, —, *Hook.*

JUNGERMANNIA, L.

1.	**Schraderi**, Mart.	On dead wood.
2.	**barbata**, Schreb.	On earth and rocks.
3.	**crenulata**, Smith.	On damp earth.
4.	**pumila**, With.	On the ground and rotting logs.
5,	**ventricosa**, Dicks.	On old logs.
6.	**Helleriana**, Nees.	Upon rotten trunks.
7.	**polita**, Nees.	Wet woody hillsides.
8.	**incisa**, Schrad.	On the ground.

SCAPANIA, Dmtr.

1.	**nemorosa**, Nees.	On damp earth.
2.	**undulata**, Nees. & Mont.	In damp places.

PLAGIOCHILA, Dmtr.

1. **porelloides**, Lindbg.
   var. **nodosa**, (Taylor.)
2. **asplenioides**, (N. & M.)   On damp earth.

To *Hepaticæ*, perhaps less attention has been given by American botanists, than to any order; it is certainly to be hoped that this neglect may not be a continuing quantity.

No classification is yet quite satisfactory, and difficulties exist, which can only be overcome by careful and long continued investigations. It would at first seem, that if *Hepaticæ* are related upon the one hand to *Musci*, and through *Ricciaceæ* upon the other hand to *Lichenes*, that a reversal of the above arrangement were called for, and that the *thallophytic* forms should be at the end of the series touching *Lichenes*, and *cormophytic* species should immediately follow *Musci*; but to quote Prof. Underwood:

"A lineal classification * * * * * does not properly present the "natural position or inter-relations of the *Hepaticæ* and other "groups, and indeed the affinities of the lower groups are too "imperfectly understood to represent even a tolerable natural, that "is to say *genetic* relationship."

This remark will apply with force to the classification of all the crytogamic orders.

Class V. THALLOPHYTÆ.

Order 110. LICHENES.

RAMALINA, Ach.

1.	rigida, Pers.	On trees.
2.	calicaris, (L.) Fr.	
	a. fraxinea, Fr.	On trees.
	b. fastigiata, Fr.	On trees.
	c. canaliculata, Fr.	On trees.
	d. farinacea, Schaer.	On rocks and trees.
3.	pollinaria, (Ach.)	On rocks.
4.	polymorpha, (Ach.)	On rocks.

CETRARIA, (Ach.) Fries.

1.	Islandica, (L.) Ach.	On the ground.
2.	aleurites, (Ach.) Th. Fr.	On trees.
	b. placorodia, Tuckerm.	On rail fences.
3.	Fendleri, Tuckerm.	On rails.
4.	ciliaris, (Ach.)	On trees and rail fences.
5.	lacunosa, Ach.	On trees and rails.
6.	glauca, (L.) Ach.	On rocks and trees.
7.	Oakesiana, Tuckerm.	In same places.
8.	juniperina, (L.) Ach.	Upon trees.

EVERNIA, (Ach.) Mann.

1.	furfuracea, (L.) Mann.	Upon trees.
2.	prunastri, (L.) Ach.	On trees and rails.

USNEA, (Dill.) Ach.

	barbata, (L.) Fr.	On trees.
	a. florida, Fr.	On trees.
	*hirta, Fr.	On trees.
	**rubigenia, Michx.	On trees.

ALECTORIA, (Ach.) Nyl.

jubata, (L.) b. chalybeiformis, Ach.   On dead wood.

THELOSCHISTES, (Norm.) Tuckerm.

1.	chrysophthalmus, (L.) Norm.	On trees, &c.
	b. flavicans, Wallr.	On trees·
2.	parietinus, (L.) Norm.	On trees near salt water.
3.	polycarpus, Ehrb.	On old fences.
4.	lychneus, Nyl.	On stones.
5.	concolor, Dicks.	On stones and trees and old fences.

PARMELIA, (Ach.) DeNot.

1.	perlata, (L.) Ach.	On trees.
2.	perforata, (Jacq.) Ach.	On rocks and trees.
3.	cetrata, Ach.	On trees and rocks.

4. crinita, Ach.   On rocks and trees.
5. tiliacea, (Hoffm.) Floerke.   On rocks and trees.
6. Borreri, Turn.   On trees and fences,and stones.
    b. rudecta, Tuckerm.   In same situation.
7. saxatilis, (L.) Fr.   On rocks and fences and trees.
8. physodes, (L.) Ach.   In similar position.
9. pertusa, (Schrank.) Schaer.   On rocks and trees.
10. colpodes, (Ach.) Nyl.   On trees.
11. olivacea, (L.) Ach.   On rocks and trees.
12. caperata, (L.) Ach.   On rocks and trees and dead wood.
13. conspera, (Ehrb.) Ach.   In same places.

PHYSCIA, (D. C.) Th. Fr.

1. speciosa, (Ach.) Nyl.   On rocks and trees.
2. hypoleuca, (Muhl.) Tuckerm.   On trees.
3. aquila, (Ach.) Nyl. b. detonsa, Tuckerm.   On rocks generally.
4. pulverulenta, (Schreb.) Nyl.   On the ground and on rocks.
5. stellaris, (L.)   On rocks and trees and fences.
6. astroidea, (Fr.) Nyl.   On trees.
7. tribacia, (Ach.) Tuckerm.   On rocks.
8. cæsia, (Hoffm.) Nyl.   On stones.
9. obscura, (Ehrb.) Nyl.   On dead wood generally.
    *endochrysa, Nyl.   On rocks and trees.
10. adglutinata, (Floerke.) Nyl.   On small trees and bushes.

PYXINE, Fr.

1. Frostii, Tuckerm.   On rocks.
2. sorediata, Fr.   On rocks.

UMBILICARIA, Hoffm.

1. Muhlenbergii, (Ach.) Tuckerm.   On rocks.
2. Dillenii, Tuckerm.   On rocks.
3. Pennsylvanica, Hoffm.   On rocks.
4. pustulata, L.   On rocks.
    b. papulosa, Tuckerm.   On rocks.

STICTA, (Schreb.) Fr.

1. amplissima, (Scop.) Mass.   On stumps and rocks.
2. aurata, (Sm.) Ach.   On ground, &c.
3. pulmonaria, (L.) Ach.   On rocks and trees.
4. quercizans, (Michx.) Ach. ?   On trees.
5. crocata, (L.) Ach.   On stumps, &c.
6. scrobiculata, (Scop.) Ach.   Without fruit, on rocks.

NEPHROMA, Ach.

1. tomentosum, (Hoffm.) Koerb.   On rocks and trees.
2. lævigatum, Ach.   On rocks and trees.

PELTIGERA, (Willd.) Fee.

1. **aphthosa,** (L.) Hoffm.   On ground and on rocks.
2. **horizontalis,** (L.) Hoffm.   On wet rocks.
3. **polydactyla,** (Neck.) Hoffm.   On ground and on rocks.
4. **rufescens,** (Neck.) Hoffm. On ground, on trunks and on rocks.
5. **canina,** (L.) Hoffm.   On ground and roots of trees.

PHYSMA, Mass.

luridum, Mont.   On rocks and fences.

PANNARIA, (Delis.) Tuckerm.

1. **microphylla,** (Sw.) Delis.   On rocks and trees.
2. **tryptophylla,** (Ach.) Mass.   On rocks.

EPHEBE, Fr., Born.

pubescens, Fr.   On rocks.

OMPHALARIA, Dur. & Mont.

phyllisca, (Wahl.) Tuckerm.   On rocks.

COLLEMA, Hoffm., Fries.

1. **pycnocarpum,** Nyl.   On tree trunks.
2. **leptaleum,** Tuckerm.   On trees.
3. **flaccidum,** Ach.   On rocks.
4. **nigrescens,** (Huds.) Ach.   On trees.
5. **ryssoleum,** Tuckerm.   On rocks.

LEPTOGIUM, Fr., Nyl.

1. **lacerum,** (Sw.) Fr.   On wet rocks.
2. **pulchellum,** (Ach.) Nyl.   On base of trees and rocks.
3. **Tremelloides,** (L. f.) Fr.   On rocks and trees in wet places.
4. **myochroum,** (Ehrb.) Tuckerm.   In similar positions.
        a. **saturninum,** Schaer.   On rocks and trees.

PLACODIUM, (D. C.) Naeg. & Hoppe.

1. **cinnabarrinum,** (Ach.) Anz.   On rocks.
2. **microphyllinum,** Tuckerm.   On old fences.
3. **aurantiacum,** (Lightf.) N. & H.   On trees and dead wood.
4. **cerinum,** (Hedw.) b. **sideritis,** Tuckerm.   On rocks.
5. **ferrugineum,** (Huds.) Hoppe.   On fences and rocks.
        b. **Pollinii.**   On trees, especially Juniperus.
5. **vitellinum,** (Ehrb.) N. & H.   On rocks and fences.

LECANORA, Ach., Tuckerm.

1. **rubina,** (Vill.) Ach.   On rocks.
2. **muralis,** (Schreb.) Schaer. a. **saxicola.**   On rocks.
3. **pallida,** (Schreb.) Schaer.   On trees and dead wood.
        c. **angulosa,** Hoffm.   On rail fences.

4. **subfusca, (L.) Ach.** On rocks and fences and trees.
    e. **distans,** Ach. On rocks and trees.
5. **atra, (Huds.) Ach.** On rocks and trees.
6. **varia, (Ehrh.) Nyl.** On trees and fences and stones.
    d. **symmicta,** Ach. In similar places.
    e. **sæpincola,** Fr. In similar places.
7. **elatina,** Ach. On dead trees.
8. **pallescens, (L.) Schaerer.** On dead wood and rocks.
9. **tartarea, (L.) Ach.** On ground and stones.
10. **cinerea, (L.) Sommerf.** On rocks.
    c. **gibbosa,** Nyl. On rocks and fences.
11. **cervina, (Pers.) Nyl.** On rocks.
12. **fuscata, (Schrad.) Th. Fr.** On rocks.
    b. **fuscescens,** Th. Fr. On rocks.
13. **privigna, (Ach.) Nyl.** On rocks.
    b. **pruinosa,** Auctt. On rocks.
    c. **Clavus,** Koerb. On rocks.

RINODINA, Mass., Tuckerm.

1. **oreina, (Ach.) Mass.** On rocks.
2. **sophodes, (Ach.) Nyl.** On rocks and fences.
    b. **atrocinerea,** Nyl. On rocks.
    d. **confragosa,** Nyl. On rocks and trees.
    e. **exigua,** Fr. On rocks and fences and trees.
3. **constans, (Nyl.) Tuckerm.** On trees and fences.

PERTUSARIA, D. C.

1. **velata, (Turn.) Nyl.** On rocks and trees.
2. **multipuncta, (Turn.) Nyl.** On trees.
3. **communis, D. C.** On rocks and trees.
4. **pustulata, (Ach.) Nyl.** On trees.
5. **leioplaca, (Ach.) Schaer.** On rocks and trees.
6. **Wulfenii, D. C.** On trees.

CONOTREMA, Tuckerm.

urceolatum, (Ach.) Tuckerm. On trees.

GYALECTA, (Ach.) Anzi.

Pineti, (Schrad.) Tuckerm. On bark of pine trees.

URCEOLARIA, (Ach.) Flot.

scruposa, Nyl. On ground.
    var. **gpysacea,** Nyl. On earth and mosses and lichens.
    var. **parasitica,** Nyl. On Cladonia.

MYRIANGIUM, Mont. & Berk.

Duræii, Mont. & Berk. On bark of Walnut trees.

CLADONIA, Hoffm.

1. alcicornis, (Lightf.) Floerke.   On light soils.
2. cariosa, (Ach.) Spreng.   On ground.
3. pyxidata, (L.) Fr.   On old stumps and ground.
4. fimbriata, (L.) Fr.   In same places.
    b. tubæformis, Fr.   In same places.
5. degenerans, Fl.   On the ground.
6. gracilis, (L.) Nyl.   On the ground.
    a. verticillata, Fr.   On the ground.
    c. elongata, Fr.   On the ground.
7. cornuta, (L.) Fr.   In Herb. Olney.
8. Papillaria, (Ehrb.) Hoffm.   On sandy soil.
9. cenotea, (Ach.) Schaer.   On old stumps.
    b. furcellata, Fr.   On old stumps and earth.
10. furcata, (Huds.) Fr.   On old logs and earth.
    a. crispata, Fr.   On the ground.
    b. racemosa, Fr.   On the ground.
    c. subulata, Fr.   On the ground.
11. rangiferina, (L.) Hoffm.   On sterile soil.
    a.   On the ground.
    b. sylvatica, L.   On the ground.
    c. alpestris, L.   On stony land.
12. uncialis, (L.) Fr.   On the ground.
    b. adunca, (Auctt.)   On the ground.
13. Boryi, Tuckerm.   On the ground.
14. cornucopioides, (L.) Fr.   On the ground.
15. macilenta, (Ehrb.) Hoffm.   On old stumps and on the earth.
16. cristatella, Tuckerm.   On rotten wood and ground.
    b. ochrocarpa.   In same places.

CYSTOCOLEUS, Thwaites.

rupestris, (Pers.) Rabenh.   *Dr. Farlow.*

BÆOMYCES, Pers., Nyl.

1. roseus, Pers.   On the earth.
2. byssoideus, (L.) Fr.   On the earth.

BIATORA, Fr.

1. exigua, (Chaub.) Fr.   On trees.
2. lucida, Fr.   Sometimes fertile, on stone walls.
3. rubella, (Ehrb.) Rabenh.   On trees.
    var. Schweinitzii, Tuckerm.
4. anthrocephala, Nyl.   On trees.

LECIDEA, (Ach.) Fr.

1. contigua, Fr.   On rocks.
2. enteroleuca, Ach.   On trees.
3. melancheima, Tuckerm.   On trees and fences.

BUELLIA, (DeNot.) Tuckerm.

1.	**atro-alba,** (Fl.) Th. Fr.	On granite rocks.
2.	**parasæma,** (Ach.) Kbr.	On trees.
3.	**myriocarpa,** (D. C.) Mudd.	On rocks ?
4.	**petræa,** (Fl.) Tuckerm.	On rocks ?
5.	**geographica,** (L.) Tuckerm.	On rocks.

OPEGRAPHA, Humb.

varia, (Pers.) Fr.   On trees and dead wood.

GRAPHIS, (Ach.) Nyl.

scripta, (L.) Sch.	On trees.
var. **limitata,** Schaer.	On trees.
var. **recta,** Schaer.	On trees.
var. **serpentina,** Schaer.	On trees.

ARTHONIA, Ach., Nyl.

pyrrhula, Nyl.   On bark of trees.

ACOLIUM, Fee., DeNot.

tigillare, (Ach.)   On old fences and rails.

CALICIUM, (Pers.) Fr.

1.	**trichiale,** Ach.	On bark of trees.
2.	**lenticulare,** (Hoffm.) Ach.	On dead wood.
3.	**trachelinum,** Ach.	On trees and dead wood.
4.	**turbinatum,** Pers.	On Pertusaria.

ENDOCARPON, Hedw., Fr.

miniatum, (L.) Schaer.	On rocks.
var. **complicatum,** Schaer.	On rocks.
var. **aquaticum,** Schaer.	On rocks.

VERRUCARIA, (Pers.) Tuckerm.

1.	**nigrescens,** Pers.	On rocks.
2.	**muralis,** Ach.	On rocks.

PYRENULA, (Ach.) Naegr. & Hoppe.

1.	**gemmata,** (Ach.) Nyl.	On trees.
2.	**nitida,** Ach.	On trees.

ORDER 111. FUNGI.

SUB-ORDER HYMENOMYCETES.

AGARICUS, Linn.

1. [Amanita] phalloides, Fr.
2. muscarius, Fr.
3. excelsus, Fr.
4. rubescens, Pers.
5. [Lepiota] procerus, Scop.
6. cristatus, Bolt.
7. granulosus, Batsch.
8. [Armillaria] melleus, Vahl.
9. [Tricholoma] sculpturatus, Fr.
10. luridus, Schaeff.
11. albus, Fr.
12. nudus, Bull.
13. humilis, Fr.
14. [Clitocybe] nebularis, Batsch.
15. elixus, Sow.
16. aggregatus, Schaeff.
17. fumosus, Pers.
18. infundibuliformis, Schaeff.
19. laccatus, Scop.
  var. amethystinus.
20. [Collybia] platyphyllus, Fr.
21. velutipes, Curtis.
22. tuberosus, Bull.
23. dryophilus, Bull.
24. [Mycena] rosellus, Fr.
25. purus, Pers.
26. lacteus, Pers.
27. galericulatus, Scop.
28. alcalinus, Fr.
29. filopes, Bull.
30. hæmatopus, Pers.
31. epipterygius, Scop.
32. citrinellus, Pers.
33. corticola, Schum.
34. capillaris, Schum.
35. [Omphalia] pyxidatus, Bull.
36. hepaticus, Batsch.
37. umbelliferus, L.
38. campanella, Batsch.
39. camptophyllus, Berk.
40. fibula, Bull.

41. [Pleurotus] ulmarius, Bull.
42.   applicatus, Batsch.
43. [Entoloma] sinuatus, Fr.
44.   clypeatus. L.
45.   rhodapolus, Fr.
46. [Clitopilus] prunulus, Scop. var. Orcella.
47. [Nolanea] pascuus, Pers.
48.   fusco-carneus, Fr.
49.   caperatus, Fr.
50. [Pholiota] durus, Bolt.
51.   præcox, Pers.
52.   mutabilis, Schaeff.
53. [Hebeloma] rimosus, Bull.
54.   lacerus, Fr.
55.   lucifugus, Fr.
56.   geophyllus, Sow.
57. [Flammula] flavidus, Schaeff.
58.   spumosus, Fr.
59. [Naucoria] ver-vacti, Fr.
60.   semiorbicularis, Bull.
61. [Galera] lateritius, Fr.
62.   tener, Schaeff.
63.   Hypnorum, Batsch.
64. [Tubaria] furfuraceus, Pers.
65. [Psalliota] arvensis, Schaeff.
66.   campestris, L.
67. [Strophania] stercorarius, Fr.
68.   semiglobatus, Batsch.
69. [Hypholoma] sublateritius, Fr.
70.   fascicularis, Huds.
71. [Psilocybe] foensecii, Pers.
72. [Panæolus] campanulatus, L.
73.   papilionaceus, Bull.
74. [Psathyrella] disseminatus, Fr.

COPRINUS, Fries.

1. comatus, Fr.
2. atramentarius, Fr.
3. fimentarius, Fr.
4. tomentosus, Fr.
5. niveus, Fr.
6. tergiversans, Fr.
7. micaceus, Fr.
8. radiatus, Fr.
9. domesticus, Fr.
10. ephemerus, Fr.
11. plicatilis, Fr.

CORTINARIUS, Fries.

1. turbinatus, Fr.
2. violaceus, Fr.
3. pholideus, Fr.
4. tabularis, Fr.
5. anomalus, Fr.
6. sanguineus, Wulf.
7. cinnamomeus, Fr.
8. castaneus, Fr.

FAVOLUS, Fries.

Canadensis, Kl.

PAXILLUS, Fries.

involutus, Fr.

HYGROPHORUS, Fries.

1. eburneus, Fr.
2. niveus, Fr.
3. lætus, Fr.
4. ceraceus, Fr.
5. coccineus, Fr.
6. cantharellus, Fr.

LACTARIUS, Fries.

1. torminosus, Fr.
2. trivialis, Fr.
3. zonarius, Fr.
4. vividus, Fr.
5. piperatus, Fr.
6. vellereus, Fr.
7. pallidus, Fr.
8. rufus, Fr.
9. volemus, Fr.
10. subdulcis, Fr.
11. fuliginosus, Fr.

RUSSULA, Fries.

1. adusta, Fr.
2. rosacea, Fr.
3. foetans, Fr.
4. nitida, Fr.
5. alutacea, Fr.

CANTHARELLUS, Adans.

1. cibarius, Fr.
2. cinnabarinus, Schwein.
3. aurantiacus, Fr.

4. umbonatus, Pers.
5. infundibuliformis, Fr.
6. cinereus, Fr.

NYCTALIS, Fries.

1. asterophora, Bull.
2. parasitica, Fr.

MARASMIUS, Fries

1. peronatus, Fr.
2. plancus, Fr.
3. fusco-purpureus, Fr.
4. archyropus, Fr.
5. calopus, Fr.
6. rotula, Fr.
7. androsaceus, Fr.
8. Olneyi, B. & C.
9. hæmatocephalus, Mont.

LENTINUS, Fries.

1. ecochleatus, Fr.
2. Le Contei, Fr.

PANUS, Fries.

stypticus, Fr.

SCHIZOPHYLLUM, Fries.

commune, Fr.

TROGIA, Fries.

crispa, Fr.

LENZITES, Fries.

1. betulina, Fr.
2. tricolor, Fr.
3. Klotzschii, Berk.
4. Sepiaria, Fr.
5. abietina, Fr.
6. Berkeleii, Lev.
7. corrugata, Kl.
8. eximia, B. & C.

BOLETUS, Fries.

1. flavidus, Fr.
2. granulatus, L.
3. bovinus, L.
4. piperatus, Bull.
5. parasiticus, Bull.
6. variegatus, Fr.
7. calopus, Fr.

8. **edulis,** Bull.
9. **luridus,** Fr.
10. **castaneus,** Bull.
11. **cyanescens,** Bull.

STROBILOMYCES, Berkeley.
strobilaceus, Berk.

POLYPORUS, Fries.

1. **[Mesopus] lentus,** Berk.
2. **leucomelas,** Pers.
3. **perennis,** Fr.
4. **brunalis,** Fr.
5. **tomentosus,** Fr.
6. **[Pleuropus] elegans,** Fr.
7. **varius,** Fr.
8. **lucidus,** Fr.
9. **Boucheanus,** Fr.
10. **[Merismus] sulfureus,** Fr.
11. **[Apus] destructor,** Fr.
12. **lacteus,** Fr.
13. **hypococcineus,** Berk.
14. **adustus,** Fr.
15. **spumeus,** Fr.
16. **benzoinus,** Fr.
17. **betulinus,** Fr.
18. **conchifer,** Schw.
19. **fomentarius,** Fr.
20. **cinnabarinus,** Fr.
21. **salicinus,** Fr.
22. **cervinus,** Pers.
23. **connatus,** Fr.
24. **radiatus,** Fr.
25. **cupulæformis,** B. & C.
26. **hirsutus,** Fr.
27. **velutinus,** Fr.
28. **zonatus,** Fr.
29. **versicolor,** Fr.
            var. **fasciatus.**
30. **laceratus,** Berk.
31. **[Resupinatus] elongatus,** Berk.
32. **Xalapensis,** Berk.
33. **pinsitus,** Fr.
34. **ferrugineus,** Fr.
35. **vaporarius,** Fr.
36. **incrustans,** B. & C.

37.   nidularis, Fr.
38.   subfuscoflavidus, Rostk.
39.   favillaceus, B. & C.

TRAMETES, Fries.

1. lactinea, Berk.
2. sepium, Berk.

DÆDALEA, Fries.

1. cinerea, Fr. ?
2. quercina, Pers.
3. unicolor, Fr.

MERULIUS, Fries.

1. tremellosus, Schrad.
2. Corium, Fr.
3. lacrymans, Fr.

FISTULINA, Bull.

hepatica, Fr.

IRPEX, Fries.

1. pityreus, B. & C.
2. cinnamomeus, Fr.
3. crassus, B. & C.
4. sinuosus, Fr.

HYDNUM, Linn.

1. imbricatum, L.
2. subsquamosum, Batsch.
3. repandum, L.
4. compactum, Pers.
5. aurantiacum, A. & S.
6. ferrugineum, Fr.
7. spadiceum, Pers.
8. zonatum, Batsch.
9. cyathiforme, Schaeff.
10. adustum, Schw.
11. erinaceum, Bull.
12. ochraceum, Pers.
13. alutaceum, Pers.
14. amplissimum, B. & C.

RADULUM, Fries.

1. molare, Fr.
2. orbiculare, Fr.
3. Bennettii, B. & C.
4. lætum, Fr.

6

PHLEBIA, Fries.

1. merismoides, Fr.
2. vaga, Fr.

KNEIFFIA, Fries.

setigera, Fr.

CRATERELLUS, Fries.

1. cornucopioides, Fr.
2. crispus, Fr.
3. sinuosus, Fr.
4. clavatus, Fr.

THELEPHORA, Fries.

1. anthocephala, Fr.
2. caryophyllea, Fr.
3. candida, Fr.
4. multipartita, Schw.
5. pallida, Schw.
6. pteruloides, B. & C.
7. laciniata, Pers.
8. sebacea, Fr.
9. cuticularis, Berk.

STEREUM, Fries.

1. purpureum, Fr.
2. hirsutum, Fr.
3. spadiceum, Fr.
4. rugosum, Fr.
5. Pini, Fr.
6. acerinum, Fr.
   var. nivosum, Curtis.
7. complicatum, Fr.
8. ochraceo-flavum, Schw.
9. Curtissii, Berk.
10. frustulosum, Fr.
11. Micheneri, B. & C.
12. albobadium, Schw.

HYMENOCHÆTE, Lev.

1. rubiginosa, Lev.
2. avellana, Lev.
3. insularis, B.
4. corrugata, Lev.

AURICULARIA, Fries.

mesenterica, Bull.

CORTICIUM, Fries.

1. salicinum, Fr.
2. Oakesii, B. & C.
3. læve, Fr.
4. viticola, Fr.
5. cæruleum, Schrad.
6. quercinum, Pers.
7. cinereum, Fr.
8. incarnatum, Fr.
9. polygonium, Pers.
10. umbrinum, Fries.
11. laxum, Fr.
12. olivaceum, Fr.
13. ferrugineum, Fr.
14. venosum, B. & Rav.
15. vagum, B. & C.
16. colliculosum, B. & C.
17. scutellatum, B. & C.

CYPHELLA, Fries.

1. fulva, B. & Rav.
2. cupulæformis, B. & Rav.

EXOBASIDIUM, Peck.

Azaleæ, Peck.

SPARASSIS, Fries.

crispa, Fr.

CLAVARIA, Linn.

1. flava, Fr.
2. botrytis, Pers.
3. fastigiata, D. C.
4. cristata, Holmsk.
5. aurea, Schaeff.
6. formosa, Pers.
7. stricta, Pers.
8. crispula, Fr.
9. fusiformis, Sow.
10. inæqualis, Müll.
11. argillacea, Fr.
12. contorta, Fr.

CALOCERA, Fries.

viscosa, Fr.

TREMELLA, Fries.

1. **foliacea,** Pers.
2. **lutescens,** Pers.
3. **mesenterica,** Retz.
4. **vesicaria,** Bull.
5. **albida,** Huds.
6. **intumescens,** Sow.
7. **torta,** Willd.

EXIDIA, Fries.

1. **glandulosa,** Fr.
2. **obliqua,** B. & C.

NÆMATELIA, Fries.

1. **nucleata,** Fr.
2. **encephala,** Fr.

DACRYMYCES, Nees.

1. **deliquescens,** B. & Br.
2. **stillatus,** Fr.
3. **chrysosperma,** B. & C.

DITIOLA, Fries.

radicata, Fr.

Sub-Order. GASTEROMYCETES.

RHIZOPOGON, Tulasne.

rubescens, Tul.

PHALLUS, Linn.

1. **impudicus,** L.
2. **duplicatus,** Bosc.

GEASTER, Mich.

1. **hygrometricus,** Pers.
2. **fornicatus,** Fr.
3. **multifidus,** Grev.

BOVISTA, Dill.

1. **plumbea,** Pers.
2. **nigrescens,** Pers.

LYCOPERDON, Tourn.

1. **pyriforme,** Schaeff.
2. **gemmatum,** Batsch.
3. **cruciatum,** Rotsk.

4. saccatum, Fr.
5. coelatum, Vahl.
6. giganteum, Batsch.

SCLERODERMA, Persoon.
1. vulgare, Fr.
2. bovista, Fr.
3. Texense, Berk.
4. verrucosum, Pers.

MITREMYCES, Schw.
lutescens, Schw.

LYCOGALA, Mich.
epidendrum, Fr.

BREFELDIA, Rostk.
maxima, (Fr.) Rostk.

RETICULARIA, Bull.
lycoperdon, Bull.

PHYSARUM, Pers.
1. cinereum, Batsch.
2. Schumacheri, Rostk.

TILMADOCHE, (Rostk.)
1. nutans, Pers.
2. mutabilis, Rostk.

DIDYMIUM, Schrad.
clavus, A. & S.

FULIGO, Persoon.
varians, Rostk.

CHONDRIODERMA, Rostk.
radiatum, Rostk.

DICTYDIUM, Schrad.
cernuum, Rostk.

ARCYRIA, Hill.
punicea, Pers.

TRICHIA, Hall.
1. fragilis, Sow.
2. chrysosperma, Bull.

HEMIARCYRIA, Persoon.
rubiformis, Pers.

CYATHUS, Persoon.
1. striatus, Hoffm.
2. vernicosus, D. C.

CRUCIBULUM, Tulasne.
vulgare, Tul.

SPHÆROBOLUS, Tode.
stellatus, Tode.

Sub-Order CONIOMYCETES.

LEPTOSTROMA, Fries.
litigiosa, Desm.

PHOMA, Fries.
1. concentricum, Desm.
2. radula, B. & C.
3. scabriusculum, B. & C.
4. nebulosum, B. & C.
5. glandicola, B. & C.
6. ampelinum, B. & C.
7. brunneitinctum, B. & C.
8. melaleucum, B. & C.

LEPTOTHYRIUM, Kunze.
1. Juglaudis, Lib.
2. Fragariæ, Lib.
3. Ribis, Lib.
4. Celastri, B. & C.
5. punctiforme, B. & C.

SPHÆROPSIS, Lev.
1. ocellata, B. & C.
2. insignis, B. & C.
3. collabens, B. & C.
4. memnia, B. & C.
5. brunneola, B. & C.
6. Gallæ, B. & C.
7. torulosa, B. & C.
8. viticola, B. & C.
9. plantaginicola, B. & C.

DISCOSIA, Lib.
alnea, Lib.

DIPLODIA, Fries.

1. viticola, Desm.
2. Rosæ, B. & C.
3. vulgaris, Lev.

DOTHIORA, Fries.

1. pyrenophora, Fr.
2. Zeæ, Sw.

VERMICULARIA, Tode.

1. circinans, Berk.
2. dematium, Lk.
3. Liliaceorum, Schw.

MELASMIA, Lev.

ulmicola, B. & C.

SEPTORIA, Fries.

1. polygonorum, Desm.
2. ochroleuca, B. & C.
3. castaneæcola, Desm.
4. Ulmi, Kze.
5. Nabali, B. & C.
6. Herbarum, B. & C.
7. maculans, B. & C.
8. plantaginicola, B. & C.
9. Rubi, B. & C.
10. Pyri, Curtis.
11. Œnotheræ, B. & C.
12. inconspicua, B. & C.
13. Stigma, B. & C.
14. complanata, B. & C.
15. Ribis, Desm.

DEPAZEA, Fries.

1. cruenta, Fr.
2. brunnea, B. & C.

DISCELLA, B. & Br.

carbonacea, B. & Br.

MELANCONIUM, Link.

1. oblongum, Berk.
2. magnum, Berk.

CORYNEUM, Kunze.

1. pulvinatum, Kze.
2. decipiens, B. & C.
3. unicolor, M. A. C.

PESTALOZZIA, DeNot.

1. Guepini, Desm.
2. unicolor, B. & C.

MYXOSPORIUM, DeNot.

nitidum, B. & C.

NÆMASPORA, Persoon.

crocea, Pers.

TORULA, Pers.

herbarum, Lk.

SEPTONEMA, Berk.

spilomeum, Berk.

SPORIDESMIUM, Link.

1. Lepraria, B. & Br.
2. melanopum, B. & Br.
3. epicoccoides, B. & C.
4. pallidum, B. & C.
5. acerosum, B. & C.
6. epiphyllum, B. & C.

PHRAGMIDIUM, Link.

1. mucronatum, Lk.
2. bulbosum, Schl.

PUCCINIA. Pers.

1. Graminis, Pers.
2. Violarum, Lk.
3. Menthæ, Pers.
4. Sorghi, Schw.
5. Polygonorum, Lk.
6. Anemones, Pers.
7. Circææ, Schw.

GYMNOSPORANGIUM, D. C.

Juniperi, Lk.

PODISOMA, Lk.

Juniperi, Fr.

USTILAGO, Link.

1. carbo, Tul.
2. urceolorum, Tul.
3. Maydis, Corda.
4. utriculosa, Fr.
5. Caricis, D. C.

UROMYCES, Lev.

1. Lespedezæ-violaceæ, Schw.
2. appendiculata, Lev.

MELAMPSORA, Cast.

salicina, Lev.

UREDO, Lev.

1. Potentillarum, D. C.
2. Solidaginis, Schw.
3. effusa, Straw.
4. Caricis, Lk.
5. Labiatarum, D. C.
6. vitellina, D. C.
7. mixta, B. & C.
8. Pyrolæ, Straw.
9. Leguminosarum, Lk.

TRICHOBASIS, Lev.

Pyrolæ, Berk.

RŒSTELIA, Reb.

lacerata, Tul.

ÆCIDIUM, Persoon.

1. Euphorbiæ, Pers.
2. Berberidis, Pers.
3. Ranunculacearum, D. C.
4. Grossulariæ. D. C.
5. Urticæ, D. C.
6. Geranii, D. C.
7. Aroidatum, Schw.
8. Compositarum, Mart.
9. Violæ, Schum.
10. rubellum, Pers.
11. Ari, Berk.
12. Menthæ, D. C.
13. Botryapites, Schw.

Sub-Order HYPHOMYCETES.

ISARIA, Fries.

brachiata, Schum.

CERATIUM, A. & S.

1. crustosum, B. & C.
2. hydnoides, A. & S.

TUBERCULARIA, Tode.

1. granulata, Pers.
2. nigricans, D. C.

FUSARIUM, Link.

lateritium, Nees.

ILLOSPORIUM, Mont.

coccineum, Fr.

EPICOCCUM, Link.

neglectum, Desm.

HELMINTHOSPORIUM, Link.

macrocarpon, Grev.

POLYTHRINCIUM, Kunze.

1. Trifolii, Kze.
2. Gallæ, Kze.

ASPERGILLUS, Mich.

glaucus, Lk.

PERONOSPORA, DeBy.

infestans, Mont.

OIDIUM, Link.

1. fructigenium, Schrad.
2. fulvum, Lk.

PENICILLUM, Link.

candidum, Lk.

DACTYLIUM, Nees.

1. dendroides, Fr.
2. roseum, Berk.

STREPTOTHRIX, Corda.

atra, B. & C.

Sub-Order PHYSOMYCETES.

MUCOR, Mich.

1. mucedo, L.
2. phycomyces, Berk.

PILOBOLUS, Tode.

crystallinus, Tode.

SAPROLEGNIA,* Kutz.

ferax, Kutz.

SUB-ORDER ASCOMYCETES.

PHYLLACTINIA, Lev.

guttata, Lev.

PODOSPHÆRIA, Kze.

Kunzei, Lev.

ERYSIPHE, Hedw.

1. Martii, Lk.
2. communis, Schl.

MORCHELLA, Dill.

1. esculenta, Pers.
2. conica, Pers.

HELVELLA, Linn.

1. crispa, Fr.
2. lacunosa, Afz.
3. elastica, Bull.
4. ephippium, Lev.

MITRULA, Fries.

1. paludosa, Fr.
2. cucullata, Fr.

LEOTIA, Hill.

lubrica, Pers.

GEOGLOSSUM, Persoon.

1. hirsutum, Pers.
2. difforme, Fr.

RHIZINA, Fries.

umbellata, Fr.

PEZIZA, Linn.

1. acetabulum, L.
2. venosa, Pers.
3. aurantia, Fr.
4. micropus, Pers.

* I have found forms of Saprolegnia upon dead fish in Benedict Pond, which appear to accord with Archer's description of S. monoica, Pringsh. and S. dioica (Pringsh.)

5. **subhirsuta**, Schw.
6. **granulata**, Bull.
7. **furfuracea**, Fr.
8. **coccinea**, Jacq.
9. **umbrata**, Fr.
10. **scutellata**, L.
11. **calyceria**, Schw.
12. **cerina**, Pers.
13. **villosa**, Pers.
14. **fusca**, Pers.
15. **flexella**, Pers.
16. **cinerea**, Batsch.
17. **atrata**, Pers.
18. **lucida**, B.

HELOTIUM, Fries.

1. **æruginosum**, Fr.
2. **citrinum**, Fr.
3. **pallescens**, Fr.
4. **herbarum**, Fr.

TYMPANIS, Tode.

1. **alnea**. Pers.
2. **conspersa**. Fr.

CENANGIUM, Fries.

1. **Cerasi**, Fr.
2. **Rubi**, Fr.

ASCOBOLUS, Tode.

furfuraceus, Pers.

BULGARIA, Fries.

1. **inquinans**, Fr.
2. **sarcodes**, Fr.

STICTIS, Persoon.

1. **radiata**, Pers.
2. **versicolor**, Fr.

CLAVICEPS, Tulasne.

purpurea, Tul.

HYSTERIUM, Tode.

1. **pulicare**, Pers.
2. **pinastri**, Schrad.
3. **juniperinum**, DeNot.

TORRUBIA, Lev.

1. militaris, Fr.
2. ophioglossoides, Tul.

HYPOCREA, Fries.

alutacea, Fr.

NECTRIA, Fr.

1. cinnabarina, Fr.
2. polythalamia, B. & C.
3. sanguinea, Fr.

XYLARIA, Fries.

1. Hypoxylon, Grev.
2. polymorpha, Grev.
3. digitata, Grev.

USTULINA, Tulasne.

vulgaris, Tul.

HYPOXYLON, Fr.

1. coccineum, Bull.
2. fuscum, Fr.
3. udum, Fr.
4. punctatum,
5. marginatum, Schw.

DOTHIDEA, Fries.

1. Ulmi, Fr.
2. Trifolii, Fr.
3. graminis, Fr.
4. Pteridis, Fr.
5. filicina, Fr.

DIATRYPE. Fries.

1. Quercina, Tul.
2. verrucæformis, Fr.
3. Stigma, Fr.

MELANCONIS, Tulasne.

Stilbostoma, Tul.

VALSA, Fr.

1. prunastri, Fr.
2. salicina, Fr.
3. nivea, Fr.

CUCURBITARIA, Gray.

elongata, Grev.

LOPHIOSTOMA, DeNot.

1. macrostomum, Fr.
2. nucula, Fr.

SPHÆRIA, Hill.

1. aquila, Fr.
2. pomiformis, Pers.
3. pulveracea, Ehr.
4. livida, Fr.
5. rubella, Pers.
6. Doliolum, Pers.
7. clypeus, Schw.
8. verbascicola, Schw.
9. ulmea, Schw.

GNOMONIA,

fimbriata, (Pers.)

SPHÆRELLA, DeNot.

1. maculæformis, Fr.
   var. æqualis.
2. punctiformis, Pers.
3. pinastri, Duby.
4. Pteridis, Desm.

MICROTHYRIUM, Desm.

1. microscopicum, Desm.
2. Smilacis, Not.

CAPNODIUM, Mont.

elongatum, B. & Desm.

DICHÆNA, Fries.

faginea, Fr.

ORDER 112. **ALGÆ.**

[*Marine.*]

SUB-ORDER CRYPTOPHYCEÆ.

GLOEOCAPSA, Kutz.
crepidinum, Thuret. Newport, *Dr. Farlow.*

LYNGBIA,* Ag.
1. **majuscula**, Harv. Providence, *Olney.* †No. 108.
2. **æstuarii**, Liebm. Narragansett Bay.
3. **luteo-fusca**, Ag. Newport, &c.
4. **tenerrima**, Thuret. Newport, *Dr. Farlow.*

SYMPLOCA, Kutz.
fasciculata, Kutz. Newport, *Dr. Farlow.*

CALOTHRIX, (Ag.) Thuret.
1. **confervicola**, Ag. Providence, &c., *Olney.* No. 112.
2. **crustacea**, (Schousb.) Born. & Thuret. Narragansett Bay.
3. **scopulorum**, Ag. Providence, *Olney.* No. 113.
  var. **vivipara**. Seaconnett, &c., *Prof. J. W. Bailey.*
4. **pulvinata**, Ag. Newport, *Dr. Farlow.*
5. **parasitica**, Thur. " "

MONOSTROMA, (Thuret.) Wittrock.
pulchrum, Farlow. Watch Hill, *Prof. Eaton.*

ULVA, (L.) Le Jolis.
1. **Lactuca**, (L.) Le Jolis.
  var. **rigida**, Le Jolis. Narragansett Bay.
  var. **Lactuca**, Le Jolis. Providence, &c.
  U. Lactuca. L. Alg. Rhod. No. 74.
  var. **latissima**, Le Jolis. Providence, &c.
  U. latissima, L. Alg. Rhod. No. 75.
2. **Enteromorpha**, (L.) Le Jolis.
  var. **lanceolata**, Le Jolis. Providence to Newport.
  var. **intestinalis**, Le Jolis. " "
  Enteromorpha intestinalis. Alg. Rhod. No. 71.
  var. **compressa**, Le Jolis.
  Enteromorpha compressa, Grev. Alg. Rhod. No. 72.
3. **clathrata**, Ag. Newport, *Olney.*
  Enteromorpha clathrata, Grev. Alg. Rhod. No. 73.

* Other species are noted under Fresh Water Algæ, p. 113.
† The No. refers to Algæ Rhodiacæ, by Stephen T. Olney, Providence, 1871; synonyms have same reference.

CHÆTOMORPHA, Kutz.

1. **ærea**, Dillw.   Newport, *Prof. J. W. Bailey.*   No. 89.
2. **Linum**, (Fl. Dan.) Kutz.
     Ch. sutoria, Berk.   Alg. Rhod.   No. 93.
3. **Olneyi**, Harv.   Little Compton, *Olney.*   No. 90.
4. **longiarticulata**, Harv.   "   "   "   No. 91.
         var. **crassior**. "   "   "   No. 92.

CLADOPHORA,* Kutz.

1. **arcta**, Dillw.   Watch Hill, *Prof. Eaton.*
2. **rupestris**, (L.) Kutz.   Newport, &c., *Olney.*   No. 83.
3. **albida**, (Huds.) Kutz.   Newport, &c., *Dr. Farlow.*
4. **refracta**, (Roth.) Aresch.   So. R. Island, *Olney.*   No. 85.
5. **glaucescens**, (Griff.) Harv. Narragansett Bay, *Olney.*   No. 84.
6. **Rudolphiana**, Ag.   Providence, *Olney.*   No. 86.
7. **gracilis**, (Griff.) Kutz.   Little Compton, *Olney.*   No. 87.
8. **fracta**, (Fl. Dan.) Kutz.   *Prof. J. W. Bailey.*   No. 88.
9. **Magdalenæ**, Harv.   Napatree Point, *Prof. Eaton.*

BULBOCOLEON, Pringsh.

piliferum, Pringsh.   Newport, *Dr. Farlow.*

SUB-ORDER PHÆOSPOREÆ.

PHYLLITIS, (Kutz.) Le Jolis.

Fascia, Kutz.   Watch Hill, *Prof. Eaton.*

SCYTOSIPHON, (Ag.) Thuret.

lomentarius, Ag.   Narragansett Bay, &c.
     Chorda lomentaria, Lyngb.   Alg. Rhod.   No. 9.

PUNCTARIA, Grev.

1. **latifolia**, Grev., var. **Zosteræ**, Le Jolis.   Providence, &c.
     P. tenuissima, Harv.   Alg. Rhod.   No. 12.
2. **plantaginea**, (Roth.) Grev.   *Pt. Judith, Olney,*   No. 13.

DESMARESTIA, Lamx.

aculeata, Lamx.   Narragansett Bay, &c.

DICTYOSIPHON, Grev.

foeniculaceus, Grev.   Narragansett Bay, *Olney.*   No. 11.

ECTOCARPUS, Lyngb.

1. **Chordariæ**, Farlow.   Newport, *Dr. Farlow.*
2. **reptans**, Cronan.   "   "
3. **granularis**, Ag.   "   "

---

*See p. 102, under Fresh Water Algæ, for other species of this genus.

4. **confervoides,** (Roth.) Le Jolis. Providence, &c.
    Ec. viridis, Harv. Alg. Rhod. No. 23.
    var. **siliculosus,** Ryellman.
    Ec. siliculosus, Lyngb. Alg. Rhod. No. 22.
5. **fasciculatus,** Harv. Narragansett Bay, *Olney.* No. 24.
6. **firmus,** Ag. Newport, *Olney.*
    Ec. littoralis, Harv. Alg. Rhod. No. 21.

SPHACELARIA, Lyngb.
radicans, (Dillw.) Harv. Newport, *Dr. Farlow.*

MYRIOTRICHIA,
clavæformis, Harv., var. **filiformis.** Newport.
    M. filiformis, Griff. Alg. Rhod. No. 20.

CLADOSTEPHUS, Ag.
verticillaris, Ag. Newport, *Olney.* No. 19.
    var. **spongiosus.** Newport, Matunuck.
    C. spongiosus. Alg. Rhod. No. 18.

ELACHISTEA, Duby.
fucicola, Fries. Narragansett Bay. No. 17.

LEATHESIA, S. F. Gray.
difformis, (L.) Aresch. Point Judith, Block Island, *Olney.*
No. 16.

CHORDARIA, Ag.
flagelliformis, Ag. Narragansett Bay, *Olney.* No. 14.

MESOGLOIA, Ag.
divaricata, Kutz. Newport, *Olney.*
    Chordaria divaricata, Ag. Alg. Rhod. No. 15.

RALFSIA, Berk.
verrucosa, Aresch. Newport, *Dr. Farlow.*

STILOPHORA, Ag.
rhizoides, Ag. South Rhode Island, *Olney.* No. 10.

CHORDA, Stackh.
filum, L. Narragansett Bay, &c. No. 8.

LAMINARIA, Lamx.
1. **longicruris,** De La Pyl. Watch Hill, *Prof. Eaton ;* Sachuest,
    Bennett.
2. **saccharina,** (L.) Lamx. South Rhode Island. No. 5.
3. **digitata,** (Turn.) Lamx. Narragansett, *Olney.* No. 6.
    7

SUB-ORDER OOSPOREÆ.

ASCOPHYLLUM, (Stackh.) Le Jolis.
nodosum, Le Jolis.
 Fucus nodosus, L. Alg. Rhod. No. 5.

FUCUS, L.
vesiculosus, L. & vars.   No. 4.

SARGASSUM, Ag.
vulgare, Ag. Rocky Point, Bristol Ferry, &c. No. 1.
 var. **Montagnei.**   Little Compton, *Olney.*
 S. Montagnei. Alg. Rhod. No. 2.

SUB-ORDER FLORIDEÆ.

TRENTEPOHLIA, (Ag.) Pringsh.
virgatula, Harv.   Napatree, *Prof. Eaton.*

PORPHYRA, Ag.
laciniata, Ag.   Newport, *Olney.* No. 69.

BANGIA, Lyngb.
fusco-purpurea, Lyngb. Narragansett Bay, &c. No. 70.

HILDENBRANDTIA, Nardo.
rosea, Kutz.   Napatree Point, *Prof. Eaton.*

NEMALION, Duby.
multifidum, Ag.   Narragansett Bay. No. 45.

SCINAIA, Bivona.
furcellata, Bivona. Newport, *Prof. J. W. Bailey.*

SPERMOTHAMNION, Aresch.
Turneri, (Ag.) Aresch.   *Olney.*
 Callithamnion Turneri, Ag. Alg. Rhod. No. 67.

CALLITHAMNION, Lyngb.
1. **Rothii,** Lyngb.   No. 68.
2. **cruciatum,** Ag.   Napatree Point, *Prof. Eaton.*
3. **Americanum,** Harv. Watch Hill, *Prof. Eaton.*
4. **plumula,** Lyngb. Newport, Block Island, *Prof. Eaton.*
5. **Borreri,** Ag. Newport, *Dr. Durkee;* Seaconnett, *Congdon.*
             No. 62.
6. **tetragonum,** Ag.   Newport, &c. No. 60.
7. **byssoideum,** Arn.   Providence, *Olney.* No. 63.
8. **corymbosum.** Providence, *Prof. J. W. Bailey.* No. 65.

9. **Baileyi**, Harv.   Newport, *Olney.*   No. 61.
10. **Dietziæ**, Hooper.   Narragansett Bay, *Olney.*   No. 64.
11. **seirospermum**, Griff.   *Prof. J. W. Bailey.*   No. 66.

GRIFFITHSIA, Ag.

Bornetiana, Farlow.   Providence, &c.
G. corallina? var. tenuis, Harv. Alg. Rhod. No. 59.

PTILOTA, Ag.

1. **elegans**, Bonnem.   Newport, *J. W. Bailey.* No. 58.
2. **serrata**, Ktz.   Block Island, *Prof. Eaton.*

CERAMIUM, Lyngb.

1. **rubrum**, Ag.   "Providence to Block Island." No. 54.
   var. **proliferum**, Ag.   Newport. No. 55.
2. **diaphanum**, Roth.   Providence, &c. No. 56.
3. **Deslongchampsii**, Ch.   Newport, *Harvey.*
4. **fastigiatum**, Harv.   Newport, &c. No. 57.
5. **tenuissimum**, (Lyngb.) Ag.   *Dr. Farlow.*

SPYRIDIA, Harv.

filamentosa, Harv.   Newport, &c.

PLYLLOPHORA, Grev.

1. **Brodiæi**, Ag.   Newport, *Dr. Farlow.*
2. **membranifolia**.   South Rhode Island, *Olney.* No. 48.

AHNFELDTIA, Fries.

plicata, Fries.   Southern shores, *Olney.* No. 49.

CYSTOCLONIUM, Kutz.

purpurascens, Kutz.   Narragansett Bay. No. 50.

CHONDRUS, Stackh.

crispus, (L.) Stackh.   Rocky ocean shores. No. 51.

RHODYMENIA, (Grev.) J. Ag.

palmata, (L.) Grev.   South Rhode Island, *Olney.* No. 46.

CORDYLECLADIA, J. Ag.

? **Huntii**, Harv.   Narragansett Bay, *Mr. Geo. Hunt.* No. 47.

EUTHORA, Ag.

cristata, J. Ag.   Newport, *J. W. Bailey;* Watch Hill, *Prof. Eaton.*

LOMENTARIA, (Gaill) Thuret.

1. **uncinata**, Menegh., v. **filiformis**.   *Prof. Harvey.*
   Chylocladia, Bailey and Harv. Alg. Rhod. No. 52.
2. **rosea**, (Harv.) Thuret.
   Chylocladia rosea, Harv. Alg. Rhod. No. 53.

CHAMPIA, (Ag.) Harv.

1. **parvula**, (Ag.) Harv.   Newport, &c.   No. 39.
2. **salicornioidea**, Ag.   Watch Hill, *Prof. Eaton.*

HYPNEA, Lamx.

musciformis, Lamx.   Narragansett Bay, &c.

POLYIDES, Ag.

rotundus, Grev.   Newport, *Prof. J. W. Bailey.*

GRINNELLIA, Harv.

Americana, Harv.   Providence, &c.   No. 42.

DELESSERIA, Lamx.

sinuosa, Lamx.   Newport, *Prof. Eaton.*

GRACILARIA, Grev.

multipartita, J. Ag.   Providence, *Prof. Harvey.*
G. multipartita, var. angustissima, Harv. Alg. Rhod. No. 43.

CHONDRIOPSIS, J. Ag.

1. **dasyphylla**, Ag.
   Chondria dasyphylla, Ag. Alg. Rhod. No. 25.
2. **tenuissima**, Ag., var. **Baileyana**.   Narragansett Pier, &c.
   Chondria Baileyana, Mont. Alg. Rhod. No. 26.

RHODOMELA, J. Ag.

subfusca, Ag., var. **gracilior**, J. Ag.   Providence.
R. subfusca, Ag. Alg. Rhod. No. 27.

POLYSIPHONIA, Grev.

1. **subtilissima**, Mont.   Providence, *Olney.*   No. 28.
2. **Olneyi**, Harv.   Providence.   No. 29.
3. **Harveyi**, Bailey.   Providence, *Dr. Farlow.*   No. 30.
4. **elongata**, Grev.   Napatree, *Prof. Eaton.*
5. **fibrillosa**, Grev.   Newport, *Prof. Harvey.*   No, 31.
6. **violacea**, Grev.   Point Judith, *Dr. Farlow.*   No. 32.
7. **variegata**, Ag.   Narragansett Bay, &c.
8. **parasitica**, Grev.   Providence, *Prof. Harvey.*   No. 33.
9. **atrorubens**, Grev.   Little Compton, *Dr. Durkee.*   No. 34.
10. **nigrescens**, Grev.   In all waters.   No. 35.
       var. **fucoides**, Ag.   Newport.
P. nigrescens, var. disticha, Harv. Alg. Rhod. No. 36.

11. **fastigiata,** Grev.   Narragansett Bay, &c.   No. 37.

DASYA, Ag.

elegans, Ag.   Providence to Block Island.   No. 38.

CORALLINA, Lamx.

officinalis, L.   Newport, &c.   No. 40.

MELOBESIA, Aresch.

pustulata, Lamx.   Narragansett Pier, *Prof. Harvey.* No. 41.

LITHOTHAMNION, Phil.

polymorphum, (L.) Aresch.   Watch Hill, *Prof. Eaton.*

The following named species of Marine Algæ mentioned by Dr. Farlow in his various works upon New England Algæ, seem to deserve insertion here, as they probably occur in our district :

Clathrocystis rosea-persicina, Cohn.   "*Whole New England coast.*"
Isactis plana, Thuret.   "*Whole New England coast.*"
Rhizoclonium riparium, Roth.   "*Probably common all along the coast.*"
Rhizoclonium tortuosum, Kutz.   "*Common all along the New England coast.*"
Bryopsis plumosa, Lamx.   "*Not uncommon all along our eastarn coast.*"
Desmarestia viridis, Lamx.   "*Common on stones.*"
Sphacelaria cirrhosa, Roth.   "*Common on Fucus.*"
Myrionema vulgare, Thur.   "*Everywhere common.*"
Asperococcus echinatus, Grev.   "*Common along the whole coast.*"
Porphyra leucosticta.   "*Probably occurs in New England.*"
Ceramium strictum, (Kutz.) Harv.   "*From New York to Cape Cod.*"
Rhabdonia tenera, Ag.   "*Common from Cape Cod southward.*"
Gelidium crinale, J. Ag.   "*Common in all seas.*"
Polysiphonia urceolata, Grev.   "*New Jersey northward.*"
Melobesia farinosa, Lamx.   "*Probably occurs throughout our limits.*"

[FRESH WATER ALGÆ.]

Sub-Order RHODOPHYCEÆ.

Batrachospermaceæ.

BATRACHOSPERMUM, Roth.

moniliforme, Roth.   Common. No. 79.
    var. **pulcherrimum**, Bory. Quidnessett, &c.
B. pulcherrimum, Hass. Alg. Rhod. No. 78.
vagum, Ag.   Davisville.

Sub-Order CHLOROPHYCEÆ.

Coleochætaceæ.

COLEOCHÆTE, Breb.

1. **soluta**, Pringsh.   Quidnessett.
2. **scutata**, Breb.   E. Greenwich.
3. **orbicularis**, Pringsh.   E. Greenwich, Spectacle Pond.

Oedogoniaceæ.

OEDOGONIUM, Lk.

1. **vernale**, (Hass.) Wittr.   Providence, *Mr. Lathrop, Olney.*
    Veseculifera Candollei, Hass. Alg. Rhod. No. 106.
2. **crispum**, (Hass.) Wittr., var. **rostellatum**, Pringsh. Prov-
        idence.
3. **paludosum**, (Hass.) Wittr.   Providence.
4. **crassum**, (Hass.) Wittr.   *Mr. Lathrop,* Providence.
5. **decipiens**, Wittr.   Providence, *Olney.*
    Veseculifera, æqualis, Hass. Alg. Rhod. No. 104.
6. **gracillimum**, Wittr. & Lund.   Providence.
7. **Lundense**, Wittr.   Providence.
8. **concatenatum**, (Hass.) Wittr.   Providence, *Olney.*
    Veseculifera, Hass. Alg. Rhod. No. 103.
9. **capillare**, (L.) Kg.   Roger Williams Park.

BULBOCHÆTE,* Ag.

1. **setigera**, (Roth.) Ag.   Everywhere common.
2. **nana**, Witt.   Mashapaug and Spectacle Ponds.
3. **pygmæa**, (Pringsh.) Wittr.   Geneva Pond.
4. **subsimplex**, Wittr.   E. Greenwich.
5. **rectangularis**, Witt.   Geneva Pond.

Sphæropleaceæ.

CYLINDROCAPSA, Reinisch.

geminella, Wolle.   Providence, &c.

Confervaceæ.

DRAPARNALDIA, Ag.

1. **glomerata**, Ag., & vars.   Common. No. 81.
2. **plumosa**, Ag.   Turns up occasionally.

* It is impossible to determine " *B. Thwaitesii. Olney n. s. Providence.*" **Alg.
Rhod.** No. 107. No drawing or description to be found.

STIGEOCLONIUM, Kg.

1. **tenue**, Kg,. a. **genuinum**, Kirch.
   S. minutum, Kg. Alg. Rhod. No. 82.
   var. **lubricum**, Rab.   Meshanticut.
2. **nanum**, (Dillw.) Kg.   Quidnessett.
3. **flagelliferum**, Kg.   Geneva.
4. **fastigiatum**, Kg.   Providence.
5. **longipilum**, Kg.   Woonasquatucket.

CHÆTOPHORA, Schrank.

1. **elegans**, Ag.   Not rare.
2. **endivæfolia**, Ag.   Providence, &c. No. 80.
   var. **linearis**, Rab.
   var. **ramosissima**, Rab.   Geneva Brook.
3. **longipila**, Kg.   Geneva.

APHANOCHÆTE, A. Br.

globosa, (Nord.) Wolle.   Quidnessett, &c.

CHROOLEPUS, Ag.

aureus, (L.) Kg.   Uncommon.

CLADOPHORA,* Kutz.

1. **glomerata**, Kg., & vars.   Common.
2. **ægagropila**, (L.) Kg.   Providence.

ULOTHRIX, Kutz.

1. **zonata**, (W. & M.) Aresch.   Common.
   Sphæroplea virescens, Berk. Alg. Rhod. No. 109.
2. **æqualis**, Kg.   Common.
   Sphærophea punctalis, Berk. Alg. Rhod. No. 110.
3. **tenuis**, Kg.   Providence, &c.
4. **subtilis**, Kg., var. **typica**.   Providence, &c.
5. **rivularis**, Kg.   Quidnessett.
6. **compacta**, Kg.   Providence.
7. **muralis**, (Ag.) Kg.   Providence.
8. **nitens**, Menegh.   Common.
9. **varia**, Kg.   Common.
10. **parietina**, (Vauch.) Kg.   Common.

CONFERVA, Link.

1. **amoena**, Kg.   Common.
2. **floccosa**, Ag.   Davisville, &c.
3. **fontinalis**, Berk.   Common.
4. **affinis**, Kg.   Common.
5. **vulgaris**, Rab.   Common.
   var. **Farlowii**, Wolle.   Geneva Pond.

* See also under Marine Algæ, p. 95.

6. **bombycina**, Ag.   Very common.
    Veseculifera, —, *Hass.* Alg. Rhod. No. 105.
7. **punctalis**, Dillw.   Common.
8. **abbreviata**, Rab.
9. **tenerrima**, Kg.   Davisville, &c.

RHIZOZLONIUM, Kg.

1. **fontinale**, Kg.   Quidnessett, &c.
2. **fluitans**, Kg.   Providence, &c.

Vaucheriaceæ.

VAUCHERIA, D. C.

1. **Thuretii**, Woron.
2. **velutina**, Ag.   *Prof. J. W. Bailey.*

Botrydiaceæ.

BOTRYDIUM, L.

granulatum, L. Newport, (*J. W. Bailey, sub, Hydrogastro.*)

Volvocaceæ.

VOLVOX, Ehrh.

globator, L.   Very common in ponds, &c.

PANDORINA, Ehrh.

morum, Bory.   Common.

EUGLENIA, Ehrh.

viridis, Ehrh.   Quidnessett, &c.

CHLAMYDOCOCCUS, A. Br.

pluvialis, A. Br.   Providence, &c.

Protococcaceæ.

PEDIASTRUM, Meyen.

1. **simplex**, Meyen, var. **duodenarius**, (Bail.) Providence.
2. **ellipticum**, Hass.   *Prof. J. W. Bailey.* No. 165.
3. **angulosum**, (Ehrh.) Menegh.   Providence, &c.
4. **forcipatum**, (Corda.) A. Br.   Spectacle Pond.
5. **Boryanum**, (Turpin,) Menegh.   Very common. No. 164.
6. **pertusum**, Kg.   Spectacle Pond, Providence, *Mr. Lathrop.*
    var. **clathratum**, A. B.   More common.
7. **Ehrenbergii**, (Corda,) A. Br.   Quite common.
    var. **cuspidatum**, A. Br.   Spectacle Pond.
    var. ?   *J. W. Bailey.*
    P. heptactis, Ralfs. Alg. Rhod. No. 163.
8. **tetras**, Ehrh.   Common.
9. **Selinæa**, Kg.   *Prof. J. W. Bailey. Desm. U. S. p.* 155.
10. **constrictum**, Hass. *Prof. J. W. Bailey. Desm. U. S. p.* 155.

COELASTRUM, Naegr.

microsporum, Naegr.   Common.

SORASTRUM, Kg.

spinulosum, Kg.   Common.

SCENEDESMUS, Meyen.

1. caudatus, Corda, var. typicus, Kirch.   Everywhere.
   S. quadricauda, Breb. Alg. Rhod. No. 166.
2. dimorphus, Kg.   Not uncommon.
3. acutus, Meyen.   Quite common.
4. obtusus, Meyen.   Quite common. No. 167.
5. rotundatus, Wood.   Providence.

OPHIOCYTIUM, Naegr.

1. cochleare, A. Br.   Very common.
2. capitatum, Wolle.   Brook at Davisville.
3. parvulum, (Berty,) A. Br.
4. circinatum, Wolle.   Quite common.
5. cuspidatum, (Bailey,) Rab.   Not common.
   Closterium, —, Bailey. Alg. Rhod. No. 161.

CHARACIUM, A. Br.

1. ambiguum, Herm.   Spectacle Pond.
2. Nægelii, A. Br.   Not uncommon.
3. heteromorphum, Reinsch.   Pocasset.

PROTOCOCCUS, Ag.

viridis, Ag.   Everywhere.
  var. angulosa, (Menegh.)   Common.
  var. dissectus, (Naegr.)   Common.
  var. miniatus, (Naegr.)   Common.
  var. infusionum, (Rab.)   Common.
  var. botryoides, (Rab.)   R. W. Park.
  var. gigas, (Kg.)   Quidnessett, &c.
  var. Wimmeri, (Rab.)   Spectacle Pond.
  var. vestitus, (Reinsch.)   Pocasset, &c.

POLYEDRIUM, Naegr.

1. trigonum, Naegr., var. bifurcatum, Wille.   Davisville.
2. gigas, Wittr.   Pocasset Pond.
3. minimum, A. Br.   Spectacle Pond, &c.
4. longispinum, (Pertz.) Rab.   Quidnessett.

Palmellaceæ.

DICTYOSPHÆRIUM, Naegr.

reniforme, Bulnh.   "Ponds now and then," rarely plentiful.

PALMODACTYLON, Naegr.

varium, Naegr.   Appears frequently.

TETRASPORA, Ag.

lubrica, (Roth.) Ag.   Providence. No. 77.
 var. lacunosa, (Chaud.)   Providence, &c.
 T. lacunosa, Chauv. Alg. Rhod. No. 76.

PALMELLA, Lyngb.

1. hyalina, Breb.   Common.
2. Mooreana, Harv.   Common.
3. uvæformis, Kg.   Geneva, &c.

PORPHYRIDIUM, Naegr.

cruentum, Naegr.   Very common.

GLOEOCYSTIS, Naegr.

ampla, Kg.   Quidnessett, &c.

NEPHROCYTIUM, Naegr.

1. Agaradhianum, Naegr.   Common.
2. Nægelii, A. Br.   Woonasquatucket, &c.

RHAPHIDIUM, Kg.

polymorphum, Fres, var. aciculare, A. Br.   Common.
 var. sigmoideum, Rab.   Common.
 var. falcatum, (Corda,) Rab.   Common.
 var. contortum, (Thur.) Wolle.   Common.

DIMORPHOCOCCUS, A. Br.

cordatus, Wolle.   Common.

EREMOSPHÆRIA, D. By.

viridis, D. By.   Stepping Stones, Cat Swamp.

Chytridieæ.

CHYTRIDIUM, A. Br.

1. minus, La Cost & Suring.   Common but not plentiful.
2. globosum, A. Br.   Roger Williams Park.

OLPIDIUM, A. Br.

ampullaceum, A. Br.   Pocasset.

Conjugatæ.

SPIROGYRA, Lk.

1. tenuissima, (Hass.) Kg.   Providence, *Mr. Lathrop.*
2. quadrata, (Hass.) Petit.   Spectacle Pond, Providence, *Mr. Lathrop.*
3. calospora, Cleve.   Providence.

4. **varians**, (Hass.) Kg.   Roger Williams Park, &c.
5. **quinina**, (Ag.)   Common.
6. **communis**, (Hass.) Kg.   Providence, &c.
   Zygnema catenæforme, Hass. Alg. Rhod. No. 95.
7. **longata**, (Vauch.) Kg., & vars.
   Zygnema malformatum, Hass. Alg. Rhod. No. 94. in part.
8. **nitida**, (Dillw.) Link.   Geneva Pond.
9. **setiformis**, (Roth.) Kg. Common in ponds; Providence,
   Mr. Lathrop.
10. **adnata**, Kg.   Providence, *Mr. Lathrop.*
11. **rivularis**, Rab.   Providence, *Mr. Lathrop.*

ZYGNEMA, Ktz.

1. **leiospermum**, D. By.   Geneva Pond.
2. **insigne**, Kg.   Providence.
   Tyndaridea, —, Hass. Alg. Rhod. No. 100.
3. **stellium**, Ag.   Common.
   var. **genuinum**, Kirch.   Common.
   var. **Vaucheria**, Ag.   Providence.
   Tyndaridea bicornis? Hass. Alg. Rhod. No. 99.
   var. **stagnale**, Ky.   Common.
4. **anomalum**, (Hass.) Kg.   Quidnesset, &c.
   var. **crassum**, Wolle.   With the typical form.

ZYGOGONIUM, Kg.

1. **pectinatum**, Kg.   Quidnessett, &c.
2. **decussatum**, (Vauch.) Kg.   Davisville Brook, &c.

MESOCARPUS, Hass.

1. **parvulus**, (Hass.) D. By.   Providence, &c. No. 101.
2. **radicans**, Kg.   Blackamore Pond, &c.
3. **nummuloides**, Hass. Providence, *Mr. Lathrop:* Pocasset, &c.

PLEUROCARPUS, A. Br.
mirabilis, A. Br.   Common.

STAUROSPERMUM, Kg.
1. **capucinum**, Kg.   Providence, &c.
2. **viride**, Kg.   Providence, *Mr. Lathrop.*

Desmidieæ.

HYALOTHECA, Ehrh.

1. **desiliens**, (Sm.) Breb.   Common. No. 114.
   var. **hians**.   Quidnessett, &c.
2. **mucosa**, (Mert.) Ralfs.   Spectacle Pond, &c. No. 115.
3. **dubia**, Kg.   Mashapaug.

BAMBUSINA, Ktz.
Brebissonii, Kg.   Common.
   Didymoprium Borreri, Ktz. Alg. Rhod. No. 117.

DESMIDIUM, Ag.

1. **cylindricum,** Grev.   Common.
   Didymoprium Grevillei, Ktz. Alg. Rhod. No. 116.
2. **Swartzii,** Ag.   Common. No. 118.
3. **Baileyi,** (Ralfs.)
   Aptogonium Baileyi, Ralfs. Alg. Rhod. No. 119.
4. **Aptogonium,** Breb.   Quidnesset.

SPHÆROZOSMA, Corda.

1. **pulchrum,** Bailey.   Davisville.
       var. **planum.**   Davisville.
       var. **inflatum.**   Davisville.
2. **filiforme,** Rab.   Spectacle Pond.
3. **excavatum,** Ralfs.   Spectacle Pond.
4. **serratum,** Bailey.   Spectacle Pond, &c.
5. **pulchellum,** (Arch.) var. **bambusioides,** Rab.   Quite
   common.

MESOTÆNIUM, Naegr.

Endlicherianum, Naegr.   Providence, &c.

SPIROTÆNIA, Breb.

1. **condensata,** Breb.   Providence, *Mr. Lathrop.*
2. **obscura,** Ralf.   Common.

PENIUM, Breb.

1. **Digitus,** (Ehrh.) Breb.   Roger Williams Park, &c.   No. 151.
2. **margaritaceum,** Breb.   Common. No. 150.
3. **interruptum,** Breb.   Providence, *Mr. Lathrop.*
4. **closterioides,** Ralfs.   Spectacle Pond, &c.
5. **truncatum,** Ralfs.   Davisville.
6. **minutum,** Cleve.   Woonasquatucket.
7. **polymorphum,** Perty.   Pocasset.
8. **Brebissonii,** (Menegh.) Ralfs.   Quidnessett.
9. **Navicula,** Breb.   Common.

CLOSTERIUM, Nitsch.

1. **juncidum,** (Ralfs.)   Common.
2. **macilentum,** Breb.   Providence. *Mr. Lathrop.*
3. **gracile,** Breb.   Providence, &c.
4. **lanceolatum,** Kg.*   Common.
5. **didymotocum,** Corda.   Providence, &c.
6. **subtile,** Breb.   Quidnessett.
7. **angustatum,** (Kg.)   Davisville, &c.
8. **Lunula,** (Ehrb.)   Providence, *Mr. Lathrop ;* Spectacle Pond.
   No. 158.
       var. **striatum.**   Providence, &c.

* A very broad form is found in Blackamore Pond.

9. **Cucumis,** Ehrh.   Common.
10. **acerosum,** (Schrank).   Pocasset, Spectecle Pond, &c.
11. **ensis,** Delpont.   Providence.
12. **turgidum,** Ehrh.   Providence, *Mr. Lathrop.*
13. **strigosum,** Ehrh.   Common.
14. **striolatum,** Ehrh.   Common. No. 160.
15. **costatum,** Corda.   Providence, &c.
16. **lineatum,** Ehrh.   Spectacle Pond, &c.
17. **areolatum,** Wood.   Rare, Spectacle Pond.
18. **Dianæ,** Ehrh.   Quidnessett, &c.
19. **acuminatum,** Kg., var. **minor.**   Providence.
20. **Jenneri,** Ralfs.   Common.
21. **Venus,** Kg.   Blackamore and Spectacle Ponds.
22. **parvulum,** Naegr.   Common.
23. **moniliferum,** Ehrh.   Spectacle Pond, &c. No. 159.
24. **Leiblinii,** Kg.   Providence, *Mr. Lathrop ;* Quidnessett, &c.
25. **rostratum,** Ehrh.   Scarce in Spectacle Pond; Providence,
    Mr. Lathrop.
26. **Kuetzingii,** Breb.   Davisville; Providence, *Mr. Lathrop.*
27. **setaceum,** Ehrh.   Providence, &c.

DOCIDIUM, Breb.

1. **crenulatum,** (Ehrh.)   Lonsdale Pond.
   D. nodulosum, Ralfs. Alg. Rhod. No. 152.
2. **Trabecula,** (Ehrh.) Naegr.   Providence, &c.
3. **truncatum,** Breb.   Providence, Quidnessett.
4. **Baculum,** (Breb.) D. By.   Common. No. 53.
5. **coronatum,** Rab.   Among Charas in Spectacle Pond.
6. **constrictum,** Bailey.   Worden's Pond; *Prof. J. W. Bailey.*
   No. 155.
7. **nodosum,** Bailey.   *Prof. J. W. Bailey.* No. 154.
8. **verrucosum,** (Bailey,) Ralfs. *Prof. J. W. Bailey.* No. 156.
9. **dilatatum,** (Cleve.) Lund.   Providence.
10. **minutum,** Ralfs.   Providence.
11. **verticillatum,** Bailey.   Worden's Pond, *Prof. J. W. Bailey,*
    Providence, &c. No. 157.
12. **gracile,** Bailey.   Providence, &c.
13. **rectum,** Delp.   Providence.
14. **Archeri,** Delp.   Spectacle Pond.

CALOCYLINDRUS, D. By.

1. **Cucurbita,** (Breb.) Kirch.   Providence.
   Cosmarium, —, Ralfs. Alg. Rhod. No. 140.
2. **curtus,** (Breb.) Kirch.   Spectacle Pond.
   *var. ? ———.   Blackamore Pond.

* This form is quite narrow, but of equal length with type.

3. **connatus,** (Breb.) Kirch. Providence.
   Cosmarium, —, *Breb.* Alg. Rhod. No. 139.
4. **pseudo-connatus,** Nord. Quidnessett.

COSMARIUM, Corda.

1. **ovale,** Ralfs. Common.
2. **Cucumis,** Cordá. Providence, *Mr. Lathrop;* Quidnessett.
3. **constrictum,** Delp. Providence.
4. **Scenedesmus,** Delp. Common.
5. **quadratum,** Ralfs. Davisville, &c.
6. **granatum,** Breb. Spectacle Pond, &c.
7. **moniliforme,** Ralfs. Neutakonkanut.
8. **globosum,** Buluh. Spectacle Pond, &c.
9. **bioculatum,** Breb. Common. No. 134.
10. **tinctum,** Ralfs. Davisville, &c.
11. **nitidulum,** DeNot. Quidnessett, &c.
12. **contractum,** Kirch. Providence, *Mr. Lathrop;* Quidnessett.
13. **sexangulare,** Lund. Neutakonkanut.
14. **depressum,** (Naegr.) Lund. Same locality.
15. **Meneghini,** Breb. Quidnessett, Providence, &c. No. 135.
16. **polygonum,** Naegr. Common, but not plentiful.
17. **notabile,** Breb. Quidnessett.
18. **undulatum,** Corda. Quidnessett, &c.
    var. **crenulatum.** Spectacle Pond, &c.
19. **crenatum,** Ralfs. Providence. No. 136.
20. **Nægelianum,** Breb. Providence.
21. **venustum,** Rab. Spectacle Pond, &c.
22. **pyramidatum,** Breb. Quidnessett, &c.
23. **pseudo-pyramidatum,** Lund. Common.
24. **Ralfsii,** Breb. Geneva Pond.
25. **galeritum,** Nord. Providence, *Mr. Lathrop.*
26. **triplicatum,** Wolle. Davisville.
27. **margaritiferum,** Menegh. Common.
28. **Botrytis,** Menegh. Common.
29. **Brebissonii,** Menegh. Quidnessett, &c.
30. **conspersum,** Ralfs. Auburn.
31. **tetraophthalmum,** (Kg.) Breb. Quidnessett, &c.
32. **intermedium,** Delp. Specracle Pond, &c.
33. **microsphinctum,** Nord. Neutakonkanut, &c.
34. **sphalerostichum,** Nord. Same locality.
35. **Portianum,** Archer. Very common.
36. **orbiculatum,** Ralfs. Spectacle Pond, &c.
37. **excavatum,** Nord. Providence, *Mr. Lathrop;* Quidnessett.

* There being no drawing, description or specimen extant, it cannot be determined what is, "C. grandituberculatum, Olney, n. sp.," Alg. Rhod., No. 141.

38. **amoenum**, Breb.   Common.
    var. **tumidum**, Wolle. Providence, &c. No. 137.
    var. **turgidum**.   Neutakonkanut, &c.
39. **Hammeri**, Reinsch.   Auburn.
40. **sublobatum**, Archer. Providence, *Mr. Lathrop*; Lonsdale
    Pond.
41. **cruciatum**, Breb.   Providence, *Mr. Lathrop*; Davisville.
42. **Phaseolus**, Breb.   Quidnessett.
43. **Schliephackianum**, Grun.   Neutakonkanut.
44. **ornatum**, Ralfs.   Spectacle Pond, &c. No. 138.
               var. **minor**,   Duck Pond, Elmwood.
45. **commisurale**, Breb.   Providence.
46. **subcrenatum**, Hautsch.   Providence, *Mr. Lathrop*.
47. **Quasillus**, Lund.   Providence.
48. **Broomei**, Thwaiter.   Quidnessett.
49. **cælatum**, Ralfs.   Common.
50. **pseudo-pectinoides**, Wolle.   Providence.

TETMEMORUS, Ralfs.

1. **lævis**, (Kg.) Ralfs.   Davisville, &c.
2. **granulatus**, Ralfs.   Providence. No. 149.
3. **Brebissonii**, (Menegh.) Ralfs.   Providence. No. 148.

XANTHIDIUM, Ehrb.

1. **armatum**, (Breb.) Ralfs.   Providence, *Mr. Lathrop*.
2. **cristatum**, (Breb.) Ralfs.   Neutakonkanut, &c.
3. **asteptum**, Nord.   Quidnessett.
4. **fasciculatum**, (Ehrb.) Ralfs.   *Prof. J. W. Bailey.*
5. **antilopæum**, (Breb.) Kg.   Common.
               var. **polymazum**, Nord.   Quidnessett, &c.

ARTHRODESMUS, Ehrb.

1. **convergens**, (Ehrb.) Ralfs.   Providence, &c.
2. **ovalis**, Wolle.   Neutakonkanut.
3. **subulatus**, Kg.   Providence, &c.
4. **Incus**, (Ehrb.) Hass.   Common.
5. **octocornis**, (Ehrb.) Hass.   Common.

EUASTRUM, Ehrb.

1. **crassum**, (Breb.) Kg.   Spectacle Pond, &c. No. 129.
2. **oblongum**, (Grev.) Ralfs.   Quidnessett, &c. No. 128.
3. **ansatum**, Ralfs.   Providence. No. 130.
               var. **major**.   Providence.
4. **pinnatum**, Ralfs.   Spectacle Pond, &c.
5. **didelta**, (Turp.) Ralfs.   Spectacle Pond, &c.

6. **ampullaceum**, Ralfs.   Providence, *Mr. Lathrop.*
7. **affine**, Ralfs.   Blackamore Pond, &c.
8. **verrucosum**, (Ehrb.) Ralfs.   *Prof. J. W. Bailey.*
9. **circulare**, (Hass.) Ralfs.   Spectacle Pond, &c.
10. **gemmatum**, (Breb.)   Spectacle Pond, &c.
11. **insigne**, Hass.   *Prof. J. W. Bailey.*
12. **Pokornyanum**, Grun.   Neutakonkanut.
13. **inerme**, Lund.   Common.
14. **cuspidatum**, Wolle.   Providence, Davisville, Woonasqua-
    tucket.
15. **Nordstedtianum**, Wolle.   Neutakonkanut.
16. **elegans**, Kg.   Providence, *Mr. Lathrop;* Neutakonkanut.
    No. 131.
17. **spinosum**, Ralfs.   Providence.
18. **simplex**, Wolle.   Providence, &c.
19. **binale**, (Turp.) Ralfs.   Providence. No. 132.

MICRASTERIAS, Ag.

1. **radiosa**, (Ag.) Ralfs.   Common. No. 121.
2. **papillifera**, Breb.   Providence.
3. **rotata**, (Grev.) Ralfs.   Spectacle Pond. No. 120.
4. **denticulata**, (Breb.) Ralfs.   Neutakonkanut.
5. **fimbriata**, (Breb.) Ralfs.   Common.
6. **furcata**, (Ag.) Ralfs.   Common. No. 123.
7. **Crux Melitensis**, Ehrb.   Quidnessett, &c. No. 124.
8. **Americana**, (Ehrb.) Kg.   Providence, &c.
9. **truncata**, (Corda.) Ralfs.   Common. No. 125.
10. **laticeps**, Nord.   Spectacle Pond, &c.
11. **oscitans**, Ralfs.   *Prof. J. W. Bailey;* Auburn, &c.
12. **pinnatifida**, (Kg.) Ralfs.   Auburn.
13. **arcuata**, Bailey.   Providence.
14. **expansa**, Bailey.   Providence.
15. **Baileyi**, Ralfs.   " Rhode Island, *Bailey.*" No. 127.
16. **foliacea**, Bailey.   Worden's Pond, *Prof. J. W. Bailey.*
    No. 126.
17. **muricata**, Bailey.   Spectacle Pond, &c.

STAURASTRUM, Meyen.

1. **muticum**, Breb., var. **minor**.   Spectacle Pond, &c.
2. **orbiculare**, (Ehrb.) Ralfs.   "Providence." No. 142.
3. **tumidum**, Breb.   Spectacle Pond.
4. **dejectum**, Breb.
            var. **mucronatum**, Ralfs.   Spectacle Pond.
            var. **convergens**, Wolle.   Common.
5. **brevispina**, Breb.   Spectacle Pond.
            var. **inerme**, Wille.   Spectacle Pond, &c.

6. **aristiferum**, Ralfs.   Neutakonkanut, &c.
7. **Avicula**, Breb.   Common.
8. **Bieneanum**, Rab., var. **ellipticum**, Wille.   Providence.
9. **margaritaceum**, Ehrb.   Common.
10. **crenatum**, Bailey. " Rhode Island, *Bailey*." R. W. Park.
11. **polymorphum**, Breb.   Spectacle Pond.
12. **crenulatum**, (Naegr.) Delp.   Common.
13. **muricatum**, Breb.   Benedict, Spectacle and Mashapaug
    Ponds.
14. **asperum**, Breb.   In same localities.
15. **rugulosum**, Breb.   Common.
16. **punctulatum**, Breb.   Providence, *Mr. Lathrop.*
17. **pygmæum**, Breb. f. **truncatum**, Wolle.   Common.
18. **alternans**, Breb.   Common.
19. **cyrtocerum**, Breb.   Common. No. 147.
20. **paradoxum**, Meyen.   Quidnessett, &c.
21. **arachne**, Ralfs.   Common.
22. **scabrum**, Breb.   Lonsdale Pond.
23. **incisum**, Wolle.   Quidnessett.
24. **cerastes**, Lund.   Spectacle Pond.
25. **gracile**, Ralfs. Providence, *Mr. Lathrop;* Spectacle Pond.
    No. 145.
26. **Ophiura**, Lund.   Common.
        var. **tetracerum**, Wolle.
        S. tetracerum, Ralfs. Alg. Rhod. No. 146.
27. **macrocerum**, Wolle.   Spectacle Pond.
28. **Rotula**, Nord.   Neutakonkanut.
29. **leptocladum**, Nord.   Providence.
30. **grallatorium**, Nord.   Common.
31. **iotanum**, Wolle.   Davisville Brook, &c.
32. **vestitum**, Ralfs.   Common.
33. **teliferum**, Ralfs.   Providence.
34. **echinatum**, Breb.   Providence.
35. **hirsutum**, (Ehrb.) Breb.   Providence, &c. No. 143.
36. **Hystrix**, Ralfs.   Providence, &c. No. 144.
37. **furcigerum**, Breb.   Quidnessett.
38. **eustephanum**, (Ehrb.) Ralfs.   Apponaug, &c.
39. **spongiosum**, Breb.   Common.
40. **arctison**, Ehrb.   Neutakonkanut.
41. **enorme**, Ralfs.   Providence.

8

Sub-Order CYANOYHPYCEÆ.

Nostocaceæ.

MASTIGONEMA, (Fisher,) Kirch.

æruginosum, (Kg.) Kirch.   Easton's Pond, Newport, &c.

GLOEOTRICHIA, Ag.

natans, Thur.   *Prof. J. W. Bailey,* sub Rivulariâ angulosâ, Roth.

RIVULARIA, Kg.

dura, Kg.   Not uncommon.

SCYTONEMA, Ag.

1. natans, Breb.   Quidnessett, &c.
2. gracile, Kg.   N. Providence.

TOLYPOTHRIX, Kg.

distorta, Kg.   Worden's Pond, *Prof. J. W. Bailey.* No. 111.

SIROSIPHON, Kg.

1. pulvinatus, Breb.   Pocasset Brook.
2. ocellatus, Kg.   Quidnessett.

HAPALOSIPHON, Naegr.

1. fuscescens, Kg.   Spectacle Pond.
2. tenuissimus, Grun.   Blackamore Pond.

NOSTOC, Vauch.

1. commune, Vauch.   Common.
2. sphæricum, Vauch.   Providence.
3. rupestre, Kg.   Providence.

ANABÆNA, Bory.

1. flos-aquæ, Kg.   Very common.
2. gigantea, Wood.   Providence, *Mr. Lathrop;* R. W. Park.
3. oscillarioides, Bory.   Roger Williams Park.

SPHÆROZYGA, (Ag.) Ralfs.

polysperma, Kg.   Spectacle Pond, &c.

LYNGBYA,* Ag. et Thuret.

1. obscura, Kg.   Pocasset.
2. vulgaris, (Kg.) Kirch.   Very common.
3. Retzii, (Ag.) Kg.   Geneva.
4. interrupta, (Kg.)   Neutakonkanut.
5. inundata, (Kg.)   Geneva.
6. Wollei, Farlow.   Providence, &c.

* See also under Marine Algæ, p. 94.

MICROCOLEUS, Desm. et Thuret.

1. terrestris, Desm. — Common.
2. anguiformis, Harv. — Geneva.
3. hyalinus, (Kg.) Kirch. — Davisville.

OSCILLARIA, Bosc.

1. subtilissima, Kg. — Common.
2. detersa, Stiz. — Roger Williams Park.
3. antliaria, Juerg. — Common.
4. leptotrichia, Kg. — Providence.
5. violacea, Wallr. — Common.
6. tenuis, Ag. — Providence, *Mr. Lathrop.*
7. nigra, Vauch. — Common,
8. princeps, Vauch. — Common.

LEPTOTHRIX, Kg.

1. tenax, Wolle. — Common.
2. cæspitosa, Kg. — Common.
3. rigidula, Kg. — Spectacle Pond.
4. bullosa, Wolle. — Quidnessett.
5. ochracea, Kg. — Very common.

ASTEROTHRIX, Kg.

Creginii, Wolle. (?) — Pocasset.

(This plant accords with Mr. Wolle's description and figure, but had not the least tinge of color.)

SPIRULINA, Lk.

Jenneri, Kg. — Quidnessett, rare.

Chroococcaceæ.

MERISMOPEDIA, Meyen.

1. glauca, Naegr. — Common; Providence, *Mr. Lathrop.*
2. convoluta, Breb. — Common.

CÆLOSPHERIUM, Naegr.

Kuetzingianum, Naegr. Common; Providence, *Mr. Lathrop.*

CLATHROCYSTIS, Henfr.

æruginosa, Henfr. — Common, at times abundant.

GOMPHOSPHÆRIA, Kg.

aponina, Kg. — Providence, &c.

APHANOCAPSA, Naegr.

Grevillei, (Hass.) Rab. — Benedict and other ponds.

CHROOCOCCUS, Naegr.

turgidus, Naegr.   Common.

*Diatomaceæ.**

EPITHEMIA, Kutz.

1. gibba, Kutz.   Providence.
2. constricta, W. S.   Rocky Point, *S. A. Briggs.*
3. **Westermanni**, Kutz.   Newport, *S. A. Briggs.*
4. turgida, Kutz.   Providence, &c.
5. granulata, Ehrb.   Providence, &c.
6. Sorex, Kutz.   Rocky Point, *S. A. Briggs.*

EUNOTEA, Ehrb.

1. tetraodon, Ehrb. Providence; Rocky Point, *S. A. Briggs.* No. 168.
2. Diadema, Ehrb.   "Providence." No. 169.

HIMANTIDIUM, Ehrb.

1. pectinale, Kutz. Providence. *Olney;* Rocky Point, *Briggs;* No. 170.
2. arcus, Ehrb.   Providence, *Olney.* No. 171.

MERIDION, (Leibl.)

1. constrictum, Ralfs. Providence, *Olney;* Rocky Point, *Briggs.* No. 172.
2. circulare, Ag.   Common.

LICMOPHORA, Ag.

1. flabellata, Grev.   Providence.
2. Pappeana, Grev.   Newport, *S. A. Briggs.*

FRAGILARIA, (Lyngb.)

1. capucina, Kutz.   Common. No. 174.
2. virescens, Ralfs.   Common. No. 176.
3. pectinalis, Ehrb.   Common. No. 175.

ASTERIONELLA, Hass.

1. formosa, Hass.   Very common in Pawtuxet water.
2. Ralfsii, Sm. ?   Meshanticut river.

NITZSCHIA, (Hass.) Smith.

Amphioxys, Ehrb.   Providence.

CERATONEIS, Ehrb.

1. longissima, Breb.   Rocky Point, *S. A. Briggs.*
2. linearis, Ehrb.   Rocky Point, *S. A. Briggs.*

---

* Diatoms follow naturally Desmids, but are removed in this list for convenience of reference to Mr. Wolle's manuals on Desmids and F. W. Algæ.

BACILLARIA, Gmel.

1. **paradoxa,** Gmelin. Newport and Rocky Point, *S. A. Briggs.*
2. **cursoria,** Dorkin. Newport, *S. A. Briggs.*

SYNEDRA, Ehrb.

1. **lunaris,** Ehrb. Providence.
2. **pulchella,** Kutz. Providence.
3. **gracilis,** Kutz. Mark Rock, *S. A. Briggs.*
4. **undulata,** Bailey. Newport, *S. A. Briggs.*
5. **Ulna,** Ehrb. Common. No. 177.
6. **splendens,** Kutz. Providence.
7. **Gallioni,** Ehrb. Rocky Point, *S. A. Briggs.*
8. **tabulata,** Kutz. Newport, *S. A. Briggs.*
9. **fulgens,** W. S. Newport, *S. A. Briggs.*
10. **crystallina,** Kutz. Rocky Point, Newport, *Briggs.*

CYMATOPLEURA, Smith.

1. **solea,** Breb. Providence.
2. **elliptica,** Breb. Providence.

SURIRELLA, (Turp.)

1. **biseriata,** Breb. Common. No. 178.
2. **splendens,** Kutz. Providence.

CAMPYLODISCUS, Ehrb.

simulans, Greg. Newport, *S. A. Briggs.*

STRIATELLA, Ag.

unipunctata, Ag. Newport, *S. A. Briggs.*

RHABDONEMA, Kutz.

1. **arcuatum,** Kutz. Newport, *S. A. Briggs.*
2. **Adriaticum,** Kutz. Newport, *S. A. Briggs.*

TABELLARIA,* Ehrb.

1. **flocculosa,** Roth. Rocky Point, *S. A. Briggs;* Quidnesset. No. 179.
2. **fenestrata,** Lyngb. Common.

GRAMMATOPHORA, Ehrb.

1. **marina,** Kutz. Newport, *S. A. Briggs.*
2. **islandica,** Grev. Rocky Point, *S. A. Briggs;* Providence, &c.

PODOSIRA, Ehrb.

hormoides, Kutz. Newport, *S. A. Briggs.*

---

* T. Thwaitesii, Olney, n. sp. allied to T. flocculosa, Providence," Alg. Rhod. No. 180, is not known by any drawing or description.

MELOSIRA, Ag.

1. **nummuloides,** Dillw.   Newport, *S. A. Briggs;* common
   elsewhere.
2. **moniliformis,** Ag.   Mark Rock, *S. A. Briggs.*
3. **sulcata,** Ehrb.   Newport, *S. A. Briggs.*
4. **granulata,** Ehrb.   Newport, *S. A. Briggs.*

STEPHANODISCUS, Ehrb.

——, sp.   Eaton Farm (fossil), *Mr. Carr.*

STEPHANOPYXIS, Ehrb.

ferax, Grev.   Newport, *S. A. Briggs.*

COSCINODISCUS, Ehrb.

lineatus, Ehrb.   Rocky Point, *S. A. Briggs.*

ACTINOPTYCHUS, Ehrb.

undulatus, Ehrb.   Newport, *S. A. Briggs.*

BIDDULPHIA, Gray.

pulchella, Gray.   Rocky Point, *S. A. Briggs, J. L. B.*

ISTHMIA, Ag.

nervosa, Kutz.   Newport, &c.

CHÆTOCEROS, Ehrb.

—— n. sp., Briggs.   Newport, *S. A. Briggs.*

SYNDENDRIUM, Ehrb.

Diadema, Ehrb.   Newport, *S. A. Briggs.*

COCCONEIS, Ehrb.

1. **dirupta,** Greg.   Rocky Point, *S. A. Briggs.*
2. **scutellum,** Ehrb.   Newport, *S. A. Briggs.*

ACHNANTHES, Bory.

1. **longipes,** Ag.   Newport, *S. A. Briggs.*
2. **brevipes,** Ag.   Rocky Point, Newport, &c., *S. A. Briggs.*
3. **subsessilis,** Kutz.   Rocky Point, *S. A. Briggs.*

CYMBELLA, (Ag.) Kutz.

gastroides, (Kutz.)   Providence, &c.

COCCONEMA, Ehrb.

1. **lanceolatum,** Ehrb.   Providence, *Olney.*   No. 181.
2. **cymbiforme,** Ehrb.   Providence, *Olney.*   No. 182.

AMPHORA, Ehrb.

1. **lævissima**, Grev.   Rocky Point, *S. A. Briggs.*
2. **robusta**, Greg.   Rocky Point, *S. A. Briggs.*
3. **affinis**, Kutz.   Rocky Point and Newport, *S. A. Briggs.*
4. **ovata**, Kutz.   Providence, &c.

SPHENELLA, Ag.

rostellata, Kutz.   Providence, *S. T. Olney.* No. 183.

GOMPHONEMA, Ag.

1. **coronatum**, Ehrb.   Providence, &c.
2. **constrictum**, Ehrb.   Providence, *Olney.* No. 184.
3. **capitatum**, Ag.   Providence.
4. **marinum**, W. S.   Newport, *S. A. Briggs;* Providence.
5. **dichotomum**, Kutz.   Providence.
6. **truncatum**, Ehrb.   Providence. No. 185.
7. **minutum**, Ag.   Providence. No. 186.
8. **gemmatum**, Ag.   Providence.

NAVICULA, (Bory,) Rab.

1. **Americana**, Ehrb.   Rocky Point, *S. A. Briggs;* Providence.
2. **didyma**, Ehrb.   Mark Rock, *S. A. Briggs.*
3. **Silicula**, Ehrb.   Quidnessett.
4. **mesolepta**, Ehrb.   Rocky Point, *S. A. Briggs.*
5. **major**, Rab.   Rocky Point, *S. A. Briggs;* Providence, &c.
6. **gibba**, Ehrb.   Rocky Point, *S. A. Briggs.*
    var. **gracilis**.   Rocky Point, *S. A. Briggs.*
7. **amphisbæna**, Bory.   Providence.
8. **Lyra**, Ehrb.   Newport, *S. A. Briggs.*
9. **Tabellaria**, Ehrb.   Providence, Rocky Point, *Briggs.*
10. **exilis**, Kutz.   Providence.
11. **affinis**, Ehrb.   Quidnessett.
12. **radiosa**, Kutz.   Providence, Rocky Point, *S. A. Briggs.*
13. **gracilis**, Ehrb.   Providence, *Olney.* No. 187.
14. **peregrina**, Ehrb.   Rocky Point, *S. A. Briggs.*
15. **viridis**, Nitzsch.   Providence, *Olney.* No. 188.

STAURONEIS, (Ehrb.) Kutz.

1. **phyllodes**, Ehrb.   Providence.
2. **phoenicenteron**, Nitzsch.   Providence, *Olney;* Rocky Point,
    S. A. Briggs. No. 189.
3. **Baileyi**, Ehrb.   Quidnessett.
4. **gracilis**, Ehrb.   Rocky Point, *S. A. Briggs.*
5. **aspera**, —.   Rocky Point, *S. A. Briggs;* Providence.

PLEUROSIGMA, Smith.

1. **Balticum,** Sm.   Newport, *S. A. Briggs.*
2. **Nubecula,** Sm.   Newport, *S. A. Briggs.*
3. **elongatum,** Sm.   Newport, *S. A. Briggs.*
4. **strigosum,** Sm.   Newport, *S. A. Briggs.*
5. **Spenceri,** Sm.   Providence.
6. **acuminatum,** Sm.   Quidnessett.

MASTOGLOIA, Thwaites.

Smithii, Thwaites.   Rocky Point, *S. A. Briggs.*

AMPHIPRORA, Ehrb.

ornata, Bail.   Providence.

DICTYOCHA, Ehrb.

aculeata, Ehrb.   Newport, *S. A. Briggs.*

DISCOPLEA, ——.

sinensis, —.   Newport, *S. A. Briggs.*

DORYPHORA, Kutz.

amphiceros, Kutz.   Newport, *S. A. Briggs.*

APPENDIX A.

ENUMERATION OF ORDERS, GENERA, SPECIES AND VARIETIES.

	No. of Gen.	No. of Sp.	No. of Vars.
Ranunculaceæ	9	28	..
Magnoliaceæ	1	1	..
Berberidaceæ	3	3	..
Nymphæaceæ	3	3	2
Sarraceniaceæ	1	1	..
Papaveraceæ	3	3	
Fumariaceæ	3	3	..
Cruciferæ	15	20	1
Resedaceæ	1	1	..
Violaceæ	1	12	2
Cistaceæ	3	7	2
Droseraceæ	1	2	..
Hypericaceæ	2	8	1
Elatinaceæ	1	1	..
Caryophyllaceæ	11	27	..
Portulacaceæ	2	2	..
Malvaceæ	3	8	
Tiliaceæ	1	1	
Linaceæ	1	4	
Geraniaceæ	4	10	
Rutaceæ	1	1	..
Anacardiaceæ	1	5	1
Vitaceæ	2	5	
Rhamnaceæ	2	2	..
Celastraceæ	1	1	..
Sapindaceæ	3	7	1
Polygalaceæ	1	8	..
Leguminosæ	18	50	1
Rosaceæ	11	41	8
Saxifragaceæ	4	6	
Grossulaceæ	2	3	
Hamamelaceæ	1	1	..
Halorageæ	3	8	3
Onagraceæ	4	12	
Melastomaceæ	1	1	
Lythraceæ	4	6	
Cucurbitaceæ	2	2	
Cactaceæ	1	1	
Ficoideæ	1	1	
Umbelliferæ	19	27	

	No. of Gen.	No. of Sp.	No. of Vars.
Araliaceæ	1	5	
Cornaceæ	2	8	
Caprifoliaceæ	6	15	..
Rubiaceæ	4	12	1
Compositæ	45	152	18
Lobeliaceæ	1	4	1
Campanulaceæ	2	3	..
Ericaceæ	16	32	3
Aquifoliaceæ	2	5	..
Ebenaceæ	1	1	
Plantaginaceæ	1	7	
Plumbaginaceæ	1	1	..
Primulaceæ	6	10	1
Lentibulaceæ	1	11	..
Orobanchaceæ	3	3	
Schrophulariaceæ	14	35	
Verbenaceæ	2	4	
Labiatæ	20	37	
Borraginaceæ	8	12	
Convolvulaceæ	3	8	..
Solanaceæ	6	14	..
Gentianaceæ	5	7	..
Apocynaceæ	1	2	..
Asclepiadaceæ	1	8	1
Oleaceæ	2	5	
Phytolaccaceæ	1	1	..
Chenopodiaceæ	6	15	2
Paronychieæ	2	2	
Amarantaceæ	2	7	
Polygonaceæ	3	28	
Lauraceæ	2	2	
Thymeleaceæ	1	1	
Santalaceæ	1	1	..
Ceratophyllaceæ	1	1	2
Podostemaceæ	1	1	..
Euphorbiaceæ	2	6	1
Urticaceæ	9	12	
Platanaceæ	1	1	
Juglandaceæ	2	8	..
Cupuliferæ	6	14	5
Myricaceæ	1	3	
Betulaceæ	2	7	..
Salicaceæ	2	20	2
Coniferæ	7	11	
Araceæ	6	7	

	No. of Gen.	No. of Sp.	No. of Vars.
Lemnaceæ	1	2	
Typhaceæ	2	4	..
Naidaceæ	5	20	3
Alismaceæ	4	8	6
Hydrocharidaceæ	2	2	..
Orchidaceæ	12	30	1
Amaryllidaceæ	1	1	
Hæmodoraceæ	2	2	
Iridaceæ	2	3	
Dioscoreaceæ	1	1	..
Smilaceæ	1	3	1
Liliaceæ	14	25	1
Juncaceæ	2	16	5
Pontederiaceæ	1	1	
Xyridaceæ	1	2	
Eriocaulonaceæ	1	1	..
Cyperaceæ	12	131	18
Gramineæ	48	126	7
Equisetaceæ	1	4	..
Filices	16	33	10
Lycopodiaceæ	3	13	
Characeæ	2	8	..
Musci	54	185	13
Hepaticæ	37	74	2
Lichenes	41	151	45
Fungi	150	582	3
Algæ	190	619	53

TOTAL.

Phanerogams...103 orders, 475 genera, 1,259 species, 101 varieties.
Cryptogams   9   "   494   "   1,669   "   129   "

      112   971   2,928   230

    3,158 species and varieties.

Twenty-two orders are each represented by one species.

251 genera of Phanerogams are represented by one species.
229   "   "   Cryptogams.

Where the typical form is not found with us, but is represented by a variety, I have esteemed that variety as a species in the above enumeration.

Of the 1,259 species of flowering plants, 200 species are *Introduced*.

APPENDIX B.

NATIVE TREES AND SHRUBS.

Liriodendron Tulipifera, L.   Local.
Berberis vulgaris, L.
Tilia Americana, L.
Zanthoxylum Americanum, Mill.   Local.
Rhus typhina, L.
    glabra, L.
    copallina, L.
    venenata, D. C.
    Toxicodendron, L.
        var. radicans.
Vitis Labrusca, L.
    æstivalis, Michx.
    cordifolia, Michx.
    riparia, Michx.   Local.
Ampelopsis quinquefolia, Michx.
Rhamnus catharticus, L.
Ceanothus Americanus, L.
Celastrus scandens, L.
Staphylea trifolia, L.   Local.
Acer Pennsylvanicum, L.   Northern part of State.
    spicatum, Lam.   Rare and local.
    saccharinum, Wang.
        var. nigrum.
    rubrum, L.
    dasycarpum, Ehrh.   Not common.
Negundo aceroides, Moench.
Prunus Americana, Marshall.   Scarce.
    maritima, Wang.   Common south of Providence.
    pumila, L.
    Pennsylvanica, L.
    Virginica, L.
    serotina, Ehrh.
Spiraea salicifolia, L.
    tomentosa, L.
Rubus odoratus, L.   Not common.
    strigosus, Michx.
    occidentalis, L.
    villosus, Ait.
    Canadensis, L.
    hispidus, L.
Rosa Carolina, L.
    lucida, Ehrh.

Cratægus coccinea, L.
        tomentosa, L., var. pyrifolia,
                var. punctata.
        Crus-Galli, L.
Pirus Americana, L.   In northern part of State.
        arbutifolia, L., var. erythro carpa.
             var. melanocarpa.
Amelanchier Canadensis, T. & G., var. Botryapium.
                        var. oblongifolia.
                        var. rotundifolia.
Ribes oxycanthoides, L.
        floridum, L.
Hamamelis Virginica, L.
Nesæa verticillata, H. B. K.
Cornus florida, L.
        circinata, L'Her.
        sericea, L.
        stolonifera, Michx.   Not common.
        paniculata, L'Her.
        alternifolia, L.
Nyssa multiflora, Wang.
Linnæa borealis, Gronov.   Rare.
Sambucus Canadensis, L.
        racemosa, L.
Diervilla trifida, Moench.
Viburnum lantanoides, Michx.   Northern part of State.
        acerifolium, L.
        dentatum, L.
        cassinoides, L.
        nudum, L.
        Lentago, L.
Lonicera coerulea, L.
        oblongifolia, Muhl.
        sempervirens, Ait.
        glauca, Hill.
Cephalanthus occidentalis, L.
Mitchella repens, L.
Gaylussacia dumosa, T. & G.   Washington County.
        frondosa, T. & G.
        resinosa, T. & G.
Vaccinium Oxycoccus, L.
        macrocarpon, Ait.
        Pennsylvanicum, Lam.
        vacillans, Solander.
        corymbosum, L. & vars.
Chiogenes hispidula, T. & G.   Rare and local.

Arctostaphylos Uva-Ursi, Spreng.
Epigaea repens, L.
Gaultheria procumbens, L.
Leucothoe racemosa, Gray.
Cassandra calyculata, Don.
Andromeda mariana, L.
        ligustrina, Muhl.
Clethra alnifolia, L.
Kalmia latifolia, L.
    angustifolia, L.
Rhododendron viscosum, Torr.
        nudiflorum, Torr.
        maximum, L.   Washington County.
        Rhodora, (L.)
Pyrola rotundifolia, L.
    elliptica, Nutt.
    chlorantha, Swartz.
    secunda, L.   Not common.
Moneses uniflora, Salisb.   Rare and local.
Chimaphila umbellata, Nutt.
    maculata, Pursh.
Ilex opaca, Ait.   Southern part of State.
    verticillata, Gray.
    laevigata, Gray.
    glabra, Gray.
Nemopanthes Canadensis, D. C.
Diospyros Virginiana, L.   Perhaps obliterate ?
Fraxinus Americana, L.
        pubescens, Lam.
        viridis, Michx. f.
        sambucifolia, Lam.
Sassafras officinale, Nees.
Lindera Benzoin, Meisner.
Dirca palustris, L.   Quite local.
Ulmus fulva, Mx.   As yet only in East Providence.
    Americana, L.
Celtis occidentalis, L.
Platanus occidentalis, L.
Juglans cinerea, L.
    nigra, L.   Whether introduced or native unknown.
Carya alba, Nutt.
    microcarpa, Nutt.
    sulcata, Nutt.   Scarce.
    tomentosa, Nutt.
    porcina, Nutt.
    amara, Nutt.

Quercus alba, L.
  obtusiloba, Michx.   Local.
  bicolor, Willd.
  Prinus, L.   ·   Local !
    var. monticola.
    var. ? humilis.
  ilicifolia, Wang.
  coccinea, Wang.
    var. tinctoria.
    var. ambigua.   Rather scarce.
  rubra, L.
    var. runcinata.   Quidnessett.
  palustris, L.   Washington County.
Castanea vesca, L., var. Americana, Mx.
Fagus ferruginea, Ait.
Corylus Americana, Walt.
  rostrata, Ait.
Ostrya Virginica, Willd.
Carpinus Americana, Michx.
Myrica Gale, L.
  cerifera, L.
  Comptonia, C. DC.
Betula lenta, L.
  lutea, Michx. f.
  alba, var. populifolia, Spach.
  papyracea, Ait.
  nigra, L.   Local.
Alnus incana, Willd.
  serrulata, Ait.
Populus tremuloides, Michx.
  grandidentata, Michx.
  monilifera, Ait. Washington County. Native ?
  balsamifera, var. candicans.
Salix tristis, Ait.
  humilis, Marshall.
  discolor, Muhl.
  sericea, Marshall.
  petiolaris, Sm.
  cordata, Muhl.
  livida, Wahl., var. occidentalis.
  lucida, Muhl.
  nigra, Marshall. & vars.
  longifolia, Muhl.
  myrtilloides, L. Found so far in Johnston only.
Pinus rigida, Miller.

Pinus resinosa, Ait.
    Strobus, L.
Picea nigra, Lk.   Not common.
Tsuga Canadensis, (Michx.)
Larix Americana, Mx.   Certainly native in W. Greenwich !
Chamæcyparis sphæroidea, Spach.
Juniperus communis, L.
      Virginiana, L.
      Sabina, L., var. procumbens.   Local.
Taxus baccata, L., var. Canadensis.   Rare and local.
Smilax rotundifolia, L., & var.
    glauca, Walt.   To the south of Providence.

www.ingramcontent.com/pod-product-compliance
Lightning Source LLC
Chambersburg PA
CBHW030605270326
41927CB00007B/1053